FACING THE GIANTS

A journey to freedom from Domestic Abuse

Comfort Dondo

Facing The Giants

copyright: Comfort Dondo 2021

ISBN: 978-1-8382081-2-7

All rights reserved.

No parts of this book may be reproduced in any form by photocopying or any electronic or mechanical means, including information storage or retrieval systems, without permission in writing from both the copyright owner and the publisher of the book.

An environmentally friendly book printed and bound in England by Diamond Publishing

Book Layout & Cover Design by Diamond Publishing

First published 2021 by Diamond Publishing, London England

Book Coach and Publishing Consultant:

Epi Mabika

www.epimabika.com

Hello@epimabika.com

DEDICATION

I would like to dedicate this book to my three beautiful children through whom I have found the strength to pull myself together, against all odds.

My beloved mother - Thank you so much for hanging on for all six of us, your children, enduring over four decades of abuse. I dedicate this book to you mama, and pay homage to every scar and pain you have had to endure.

Last but not least - All the women I have had the privilege to work with over the years, including some who have lost their lives. I dedicate these writings to you, with the hope that you are still on your healing path. May you ensure that all the young people in your lives get a hold of a book like this one, so that we can create a violent-free and peaceful generation to come.

ACKNOWLEDGEMENTS

My late father, the man I had a complicated relationship with since in utero. A lot of my life lessons were drawn from him, for it was through my interactions with him that I began questioning a lot of intolerable behaviours, and began to choose what I wanted and did not want from my life.

My great friend and brother Apostle T.F Chiwenga. Thank you for being a constant reminder of the love of God and the millions of hours of outpouring love you have for me as a friend and sister. Some of the nights or early mornings that I call you when I experience a major anxiety attack, I am amazed by your selflessness in giving much love and support to me.

Mandy Iverson, St Catherine University Director of Alumni Relations, thank you for your support.

St Catherine University, I want to pay homage to the school and space that moulded me to knowing myself and that taught me to lead and influence. Thank you, for most of who I am today as an adult, is because of you.

To Epi Mabika - The Queen, sister friend and Professional Book Coach who has made this dream possible - Thank you! You are my God assigned Doula for this book as you have made it come alive by pulling it out of me. Even when I stalled, because writing about your pain is hard, you were patient with me, holding my hand to guide and encourage me. You are one of the most proficient coaches I have ever worked with and I am so grateful and so inspired by you.

vii

Contents

DEDICATION	v
ACKNOWLEDGEMENTS	vii
PREFACE	xi
INTRODUCTION	13
CHAPTER 1	18
THE STOLEN VOICE	19
A day of a thousand emotions	19
Instruments of terror	22
A False Escape	25
Dear Younger Me	28
CHAPTER 2	32
GROWING PAINS	33
The Warzone	33
The dichotomy of life	38
The Tragic impacts of Trauma	42
Cultural Toxicity	47
CHAPTER 3	52
FROM POT TO FIRE	53
Grown-ish	53
Issues in my tissues	59
Sizing Up	64
Victim or Victor	69
CHAPTER 4	76
BORN A CRIME	77
The Criminal Justice System	77
Me against the world	81

The cycle continues	85
Oasis in the Desert	89
CHAPTER 5	**92**
KNOWING THE TRAITS	**93**
Mr Charming can also be Mr Harming	93
Spotting the Red Flags	99
Cycles of Abuse	106
Turning Red Flags into White	110
CHAPTER 6	**116**
ABUSE	**117**
The intangible enemy	117
Exposing Physical and Sexual abuse	122
Highlighting Emotional and Verbal Abuse	125
Uncovering Financial and Social media Abuse	130
CHAPTER 7	**138**
HEALING FOR WHOLENESS	**139**
Healing past wounds	139
The secret to Overcoming	145
Adversity to advantage	151
Phoenix Rising	154
CHAPTER 8	**158**
A NEW BEGINNING	**159**
JOURNAL	**161**
BOOK CONCLUSION	**177**

PREFACE

Domestic Violence - the real pandemic that has been plaguing homes since the beginning of time...

According to the World Health Organization (WHO):

- Violence against women – particularly intimate partner violence and sexual violence – is a major public health problem and a violation of women's human rights.

- Estimates published by WHO indicate that globally about 1 in 3 (30%) of women worldwide have been subjected to either physical and/or sexual intimate partner violence or non-partner sexual violence in their lifetime.

- Most of this violence is intimate partner violence. Worldwide, almost one third (27%) of women aged 15-49 years who have been in a relationship report that they have been subjected to some form of physical and/or sexual violence by their intimate partner or known relative.

- Violence can negatively affect women's physical, mental, sexual, and reproductive health, and may increase the risk of acquiring HIV in some settings.

- Violence against women is preventable. The health sector has an important role to play to provide comprehensive health care to women subjected to violence, and as an entry point for referring women to other support services they may need.

INTRODUCTION

I survived, though not without some scars. My scars tell a story. They are a reminder of times when life tried to break me, but failed. They are the markings of where the structure of my character was carved.

In these pages I will open up about the darkness and depravity of domestic violence and sexual abuse, to dismantle the calcified cracks and bleeding silence. I want to expose the darkness to parents, so that terrified children will be set free. I want to expose this cruel practice to the world, so that vulnerable women and men can break free from these binding chains. Perpetrators should no longer be able to hide in the shadows, but instead be brought into light for justice and accountability. As the glass walls of abuse shatter around the victim, I hope that this book leads to a path of forgiveness and healing for both the victim and the perpetrator. It is only through exposing painful truths that we can ever change the face of sexual, physical and verbal abuse. These are epidemics of global proportions that have been the real pandemic, plaguing homes since the beginning of time.

Much of what is expressed here pertains to my own personal growth, from a survivor of childhood sexual abuse to a child who grew up in a violent home, and eventually an adult survivor of both domestic and systemic violence. I have come to realise that silent tears hold the loudest pain. I wanted to find a way to silently crawl out of my shame, but on my knees, I discovered a pathway that would instead lead me to my voice and give me wings. Sometimes God will use your deepest pain to launch your greatest calling. Today I am flying high and thriving. I have become unstoppable! As a women's rights' advocate and recovering victim, each survivor I come in contact with has been a mirror to my own self, where I reflect on my own journey. One of the main themes that prompted me to write this book is how victimhood is largely due to how we hang on to that label, rather than setting ourselves free. We hold on to that identity, sometimes long after the abuse has occurred. Many of us have handicapped and victimized ourselves by belief systems that others have instilled upon us. One example from my life is when I conquered anxiety. I even called it, "my anxiety", before I healed and started to operate from a place of healing and strength. Hanging on to my anxiety meant living up to this label, which had given me a lot of reasons to avoid confronting hard situations in my life. In addition to this, I also numbed out things I was not comfortable dealing with. I came to realise that the residue of my childhood trauma was bleeding into my adulthood and making decisions for me from an unhealthy place.

This book is dedicated to my mother and children. A lot of the examples come from my own life experience with a message in it for you, yet in many ways, still for me as well. I hope that as you read it, you will enjoy, learn, grow, escape, become bold, but most of all, you rise to become the queen and king of your own life - taking charge, from victim to victor.

What I write in this book is based on the central belief that all people are created equal and every human has the right to free will and to choose what their spirit leads them to - as long as they are not infringing on another person's rights.

If you have ever felt that your life is controlled by other forces besides you, this book is for you. Each person's life is unique, separated from any other individual by personal experiences. No one else can live your life, nor be in your shoes to fully understand your personal experience. It is my desire that after reading this manual, you are able to claim back your power, and achieve total control over your own life. It's time to disentangle yourself and put on a new identity. No one can take care of your life as well as you.

Each chapter will take you through concrete steps to help you adopt and implement your own healthy mindset that will release you from the strongholds of abuse and domestic violence. This is a whole process that doesn't happen overnight - it takes time.

When we look at nature and other living creatures, we find that they have a lot to teach us about this process of life. Maya Angelou put it this way, "We delight in the beauty of the butterfly, but rarely admit the changes it has gone through in order to achieve that beauty."

This process called Metamorphosis isn't just some beautiful physical transformation. It is a stunning display of evolutionary mechanisms at work. Butterflies and caterpillars don't just look different, they behave differently too. One lives in trees, and the other one flies. Most importantly - one eats leaves, and the other solely feeds on nectar... the sweet stuff.

There's plenty of room for both kinds to coexist in the ecosystem since they don't interfere with each other's food stocks. However, transformation is not pretty. It is a gruesome process, and people tend to forget that this beautiful delicate butterfly once used to hang on all 12 legs, eating dirty leaves. There was not much beauty there. People talk about caterpillars becoming butterflies as though they just go into a cocoon, slap on some wings and they are good to go. No! Caterpillars have to dissolve into a disgusting pile of grime to become a beautiful butterfly that's free to fly wherever it pleases and feed on the sweet nectar of success. It takes a whole process. So if you are in a mess, entangled in all sorts of cocoons and nasty challenges, keep going.... the end will be beautiful.

You will be broken if you don't take the time to love yourself first and rebuild your self-esteem. You will be broken as long as you allow yourself to be broken. As your self-worth begins to blossom, all of the excruciating pain you are feeling will slowly fade away. In the same way that you cannot heal in the same environment that made you sick, you cannot heal with the same mindset and perspective that is keeping you in bondage. It's time to change your thinking 'environment', through my story and the tools that I will provide for you. These will set you free and allow you to begin to heal.

As I am stronger enough now, I can gracefully show my scars, not my bleeding wounds. Scars show us where we have been - they do not dictate where we are going. As a soldier returning from a vicious and victorious battle, I wear my scars like stripes with pride because they have given me a higher ranking to fight any battle with authority and overcome with confidence. Come on this journey with me and meet my heart on paper.

CHAPTER 1

THE STOLEN VOICE

A day of a thousand emotions

"Scream, and I will kill you!", he uttered harshly under his breath as he took treacherous actions against my innocent virgin body. As he lusted against me, I could still hear the laughter and excitement of the adults in the living room - still enjoying the brand new color television that had brought us all so much joy that day. All the people that would have protected me were right there in the next room…. yet, I was totally defenseless.

My little confused nine-year-old mind could not fathom what was happening…. You see, just a few moments earlier, we were all elated as my uncle who was relocating back from Australia had returned home that very day. Having lived abroad with his wife for several years, he had now decided that he had paid his dues and wanted to settle back amongst his own people in his country of origin.

Amidst the sheer jubilation in the home at his arrival, we were completely outdone when he pulled out a large box, gifting it to the whole family. Our mouths dropped as he opened the box to our first ever color television. This was in the early 80's, and owning a TV was such a big deal, let alone a colour TV for that matter! This was an emblem of wealth at the time, signifying that one had made it in life. Everyone in the neighbourhood would know and marvel at the sheer thought of owning an actual TV. For us, it was like Christmas had exploded on an ordinary day. The squeals of joy and excitement are ones that I will never forget. We all stood around with mouths dropped, admiring the latest Technicolor Marvel that was rare in our area.

With help from a step-uncle who lived with us, the TV was assembled together, as we watched from the edge of the sofa. When it came glowing to life, we were glued and mesmerised by the constant flow of colorful images. Mother provided a gratitude ritual with her signature food and drinks to mark the occasion. It was so nice sitting together, content with family and a television that would bring us years of unending happiness. We ate and talked under the chatter of the television until it got late. Mother quietly nodded for us children to go to bed. She was a stickler for a consistent bedtime. Being a teacher, she would always lecture us on the five benefits of kids getting more than enough sleep. "Sleep is important," she used to say, "sleep helps you grow"... and on and on she would go, stating her case as if we cared to know. If we heard it once, we heard it a thousand times and we would just roll our eyes behind her back. When she mentioned the magical words, "Lights out"... we all filed out obediently.

Not long after I had tugged the covers above my head, I heard my bedroom door open slowly. I was surprised to see that

20

it was my step-uncle who had come into my room, closing the door behind him. Something wasn't right, the men generally didn't enter the girls' rooms, yet he was a trusted member of our family who lived with us and even worked for my father. 'Maybe he was just coming to say goodnight or wanted to know what I thought about the new television', I thought to myself.

It wasn't until he slipped onto the bed and covered my mouth, that abject horror filled my little nine-year-old soul as he uttered those chilling words... "Scream, and I will kill you!"

Instruments of terror

The hand is not something that most people think about. We use our hands every day, never realizing how powerful they really are in life. From the gentle touch of a mother when a newborn baby is laid on her bosom, to the squeeze of the hand from one departing this world, the power of touch is more potent than we can ever imagine. The hand for me symbolizes caring, positive aspects and phrases associated with it for instance, 'Extend a hand of friendship'; 'Take my hand in marriage'; 'Hand-in-hand with my best friend'; 'The work of our hands is blessed'; 'The hand of God is upon us'... and so on. Hands are meant to be instruments of good works. Each finger on a hand is important, despite having unique functions and roles: The thumb, pointer, middle, ring and baby finger, each have different a function and purpose on the same hand, yet when they come together in unison, they are symbolic of prayer, gift-giving or clapping to celebrate good things.

In contrast to this however, one must think about the duality of all existence. As Myles Munroe put it, 'When the purpose of a thing is not known, abuse is inevitable'.

Take fire for example - it is used to warm up a home during long winter nights, and also prepare our daily meals, yet the same fire can burn the same house down, and can even consume a whole forest.

Hands also have this dual existence. For all the comfort that hands can bring, the pain can be equally searing. It doesn't take but one wrong touch of a hand to shatter innocence and set our lives on a collision course of immeasurable pain and difficulty.

When I think of the of the analogy of hands, I am reminded of the harsh reality that those people who are supposed to care for and nurture your children, often living in the same home and community, most times end up using these same hands to cause despicable harm and doing the very opposite of nurturing to our children.

Hands are meant to be instruments of good works - as a mother holds her new born baby, she uses her hands to tend, feed and nurture the baby until they are independent enough to be on their own.

The opposite baffles me, on how hands are also used to invoke pain, destruction, abuse and life changing damage. To think that a whole human being can deliberately choose to abuse that original purpose of hands by slapping, gagging, violating and worse still, choking another human being with these very same instruments is totally absurd!

For me, the same hands that had just brought me such exhilarating joy in helping to unwrap and assemble the big TV gift that very night, were now poised on my body to destroy my innocence. There are no words to describe the panic, confusion and terror that was engulfing me.

The hands that had once brought me happiness, now crushed me with hate, plunging my life into a world of silence as his threat to kill me hung tangibly over my head. Disillusioned, disgusted and dismayed, I lay there obliterated in pain, as the violence tore through my tiny helpless body. I could never look at his hands the same again. They would no longer be instruments of love, but of terror.

That night began an eight-year journey into hell, as I was forced to painfully and silently coexist with my molester. My step-uncle never moved out of our home after these horrific experiences, which I would later learn were actually sexual assault. He even took a job at my father's butchery. The sheer narcissism was beyond belief.

A False Escape

Life after the sexual abuse was a hazy and sometimes foggy childhood. Research allowed me to understand how the brain protects you from experiencing pain by compartmentalizing the painful experiences. In some ways, it gives you a false sense of amnesia. I call it a false sense of forgetting the trauma because subconsciously, the pain shows up and manifests in other ways including anger, anxiety and disruption in forming trusting healthy relationships.

In other words, it creates a false sense of escape by dealing with the fruit, rather than the root of the problem. Like nasty weeds however, the fruit will always grow again until the whole tree is uprooted.

My performance in school was never impacted by the trauma I experienced both in a violent home environment and staying with my abuser. I somehow managed to tuck away the pain and get on with my day. In fact, it made me focus more on school to stay preoccupied. I kept to myself as I was never, and still to this day not quick to make friendships. Having trusting healthy relationships has been one of the parts of myself I have had to work hard to acquire through healing myself.

Contrary to this however, many people think I am an extrovert because of how I show up in my work today as an advocate, activist and social entrepreneur. I am in fact introverted and shy, and I wonder if this part of my personality was natural, or just my coping mechanism to keep safe from being hurt.

The famous actor, producer and billionaire mogul - Tyler Perry, credits his creativity to a similar process of escapism where he would create an alternate reality in his mind in order to escape the reality of his abusive and alcohol-addicted father towards him and his mother. This was his coping mechanism as a child, before going through therapy to face and deal with the reality of the trauma to find true healing.

Lately, I have been giving excuses on why I work long hours and my only close friends are my three children, but truth be told, I have always had a difficult time making and keeping genuine friends. My childhood taught me to create some protective walls around myself, where I do not want to bring people too close. With the few times I have tried to create close friendships, some have resulted in betrayal. To this I will not claim victimhood - I believe you attract who you are. So before I began my healing journey, I was hurting, and as you know, hurt people hurt others also.

As they say, misery loves company, so I gathered the company of fellow miserable, hurting people that I would later discover were not true friends at all.

I had to take full ownership for the part I played in broken friendships, and began to heal. Until you pursue that long and uncomfortable journey of healing childhood wounds, everything you will attract to yourself will continue to be a mirror of your pain and a reflection of who you are.

I would love to share that after my healing journey, I became comfortable with being alone, and had the liberty to hand pick healthy nourishing people I wanted in my circles. This was a game changer because my life became healthier and enriched as a result of this.

I felt it significantly important at this point to speak to the little girl I have neglected for far too long over so many years. Hidden under a faceless mask and buried too deep in a grave full of skeletons, I wasn't willing to confront her before this moment. Whilst my adult self was busy living her life, the little girl inside me was still waiting for me to come back to her and rescue her. I became good at compartmentalizing my life, putting that little girl in a box and keeping her locked up in a junk garage somewhere in Harare. I was good at escaping and distancing myself from the past, only to realize that it is the piece of me that completes the puzzle of who I am today. I am now realizing that the past shouldn't be something that haunts you, but instead propels you further like the eagle in the storm, using that very same wind to glide you to a higher purpose for your present benefit. The past helps you to recognize and appreciate how far you've come and as Nelson Mandela put it, "There is nothing like returning to a place that remains unchanged to find the ways in which you yourself have altered."

Dear Younger Me

I share this letter with you, as I found it very cathartic to write to my younger self as part of the healing journey and the release I so desperately sought through life's trinkets, pleasures and all the wrong people.... only to finally realise that indeed 'younger me' holds so many answers to many questions in my life - the key that would finally release me from the dungeons and imprisonment of domestic abuse. So I have decided to go through this journey with her, and I invite you to join me as I write a letter to her.

Dear Younger me...

Hello my Dear Comfort, my dear nine-year old self. I know this letter is long overdue, but I finally plucked up the courage to speak to you. I know that all these years you've been waiting for me to come and sit with you. Thank you for waiting for me....

I am coming back to you. I have been seeing more and more of you show up, since I stopped muting your voice. Thank you for your patience with me because for a whole decade, I had decided to numb you out, as that was the only way I thought I could function.

After experiencing some insecurity earlier this year, I decided I was either going to live fully, or die! For me, living was going to include allowing myself to bring you back from the shelf I had long placed you. I see more and more of you now, maybe because I am allowing myself to feel you. Sometimes I think it's because I am seeing bits and pieces of you through my children.

The other night, my son and I were watching one of my favourite childhood bible stories about Queen Esther, and you showed up. It reminded me of the few moments I recall you feeling safe, and this was when mom shared bible stories with you then prayed. Of course, this was before the nights when dad showed up angry and all hell broke loose.

Again, on my last trip to Dubai I experienced your visitation when I was feeling unsafe during a taxi ride to the Hotel. Almost as if in a trance, I realized that shelving you was creating the same patterns of abuse, and attracting the same toxic situations in my life, so I decided to come back to you.

In my mother's garden, that one last night in Zimbabwe, when I would imagine leaving you for good - the nine year old girl who was violated, with feelings of being dirty, unlovable and in my father's own words "mahure!"(meaning prostitutes) - these are the things I wanted to leave behind and start anew, but I couldn't.

Maybe I left the 'idea' of these painful things, but this year, I made a bold move towards my health - to stop taking numbing medication or chemicals, so I could reach back to you where I had left you. I realized that until I heal you and the wounds I attempted to leave behind, I would continue to chase a rabbit hole, and end up in the same situation.... back to nowhere.

Dear baby girl, I came back for you, to take you along with me back to the States, where I am now an adult. In so many ways, I'm learning to be part of you again - a kid, raising my own three children. I would love you to join me on this beautiful journey.

I need you to know that I never wanted to abandon you for this long, but the idea of feeling and dealing with the pain scared me. I had other pressing issues, like homelessness, no food at times, and even more rejection like when I was pregnant with my first child.

So I had to just sit on that glass bottle and keep numbing the pain. For a moment, it took the anxiety and edge off, but each morning you showed up all the way from wherever I had buried you and softly whispered in my ear. I would feel guilty all day, only to sip again at night, to try and drown out the sorrows. So the cycle continued, but now I am ready to hear what you have to say.

Here we are, I am so happy you waited. I would love to have you join me and be present here with me. You are welcome here, because it is safe now. I want to nurture you and heal with you, because you are me, my very foundation.

I am happy to feel you again and every day, it's a major win just to feel you again.

I will protect you and be here for you, until we heal together. For it will be in the healing not the wounds, that we will thrive.

I hope to get your love, in this healing not just of me, but many women. So many women will need you and me to work together, to help them locate their little girls, and bring them forth to heal them.

Now hold my hand and walk with me. Do not be afraid, for I am here to protect you. I will always stand up for you. I will speak up for you. I will use my voice for you. You make up an important part of who I am. I have grown into this beautiful woman because you were strong enough not to give up on life. No matter how difficult it became, you were still here waiting for me. Now I am here. Let's take this journey together. Our destiny awaits, and I want you to be part of it. So many people are waiting to be inspired by you.

With the beautiful Hawaiian Prayer for Forgiveness, Ho'oponopono which roughly translates to "cause things to move back in balance and make things right", I am giving you back your voice today and I say this to you...

I'M SORRY.

PLEASE FORGIVE ME

I'M HERE NOW

THANK YOU

I LOVE YOU

LET'S DO THIS TOGETHER

Signed... Comfort Dondo (2021)

CHAPTER 2

GROWING PAINS

The Warzone

On the one hand, the opportunities for a happy childhood experience were plenty, yet on the other hand, all these horrific encounters were happening to me - a perplexing paradox all happening at the same time.

I remember as if it were yesterday, residing in our small home in a small township on the outskirts of Zimbabwe's capital city Harare - a wonderful place to live and grow up in, despite the poverty and high HIV rates that surrounded my township. On any given day, we had the best of times, making up silly games with other neighborhood kids. It was normal to see us lost in our own little worlds, enjoying nature as we would dash out into the monsoon rain with soap on our heads to get the best shower in the world ever!

Everyone worked hard for the things that they proudly loved. It was the world that defined poverty to me, but as far as I was concerned we were rich in everything that mattered.

It wasn't your typical perfect pretty 'white picket fence' cul-de-sac, however it was a place that I was happy to be in despite the numerous difficulties surrounding my little small township.

Growing up in a small township of Chizhanje Mabvuku in Harare, was an experience I wished that all my affluent friends would have had. According to outsiders, we were poor and our homes were too small, but there was an invisible richness and depth to my community that no amount of money or wealth could achieve.

In our community, we were and still are each other's keeper. I remember my mother sending me to all the widows in the neighborhood. There were at least two on each road with at least seven main streets that I would deliver some meat - beef, liver and goat meat, salt, spices and mealie meal. Around Christmas time I would deliver the extra special - Chicken pieces and rice. Chicken was considered a luxury and 'THE Christmas meal' in those days. Those that didn't have chicken for christmas, were considered extra poor and would become a laughing stock.

However, we were community focused with lots of love for each other. This was typical in my neighborhood. At times we would also indulge in looming folktales about which old women to avoid - those who were called 'the witches'. There were a few that no matter how much food they would offer me, I would take it and just throw it in the bins because their danger of witchcraft was ingrained in me.

In spite of all this, I didn't have lots of real friends and preferred to spend my time in the library. Since we did not have any near my house, I would walk at least seven miles each way to go to the nearest City Council library, which I out-read by the time I was in Grade 5. By Grade 6, I asked my parents to give me transportation money to go to the bigger Library in the main Capital City. I would buy lunch on my way, read and take lunch breaks and continue to read.

Books became the only consistent friend with whom I could confide in and disappear from my reality. This was my coping mechanism which provided a safe and great escape for me.

It was my love for books that continues to serve me to date.

As horrific as it was to be raped by my step-uncle during those years, he was not my only abuser. Multiple abuses are far more common than you may think, and they are carried out by both genders... on both genders!

Another 'trusted woman' that abused me, plunged my life into unimaginable darkness and depression. I will never be able to express the feeling of helplessness and those mind warping experiences into words. Yet inwardly I knew that I had to stay strong despite my devastation. I learned that I had to grow up quickly. My sole goal in life was to escape the abuse. I was determined to create opportunities for myself.

Any kind of violation that occurs to one as a minor child, completely changes the normal flow of growth in that person. I would like to say from as young as nine years old, my life felt like there was a huge Tiger sitting on my chest each day. I was fighting an invisible monster in silence, and I had to make the choice of either fighting or fleeing.

This created a war zone around me, and I became very good at both.

Zimbabwe is a highly patriarchal society, one in which the girl child is objectified and in some ways, groomed early for marriage as the only goal in life. In addition to this, there is the typical 'name calling' and undermining of women by men - that which I personally experienced from both my father and random males around me. From this young age, I learned to teach males how to treat me.

I learned to fight both with my words and physically as well sometimes because I would have to walk at least 2 miles from the bus station to my parent's house alone, coming from the library.

Boys and young men would feel the need to pass any comments, based on what girls were wearing or the numbers that were present in the group. I used to stand there and fight back with my words, usually letting them know I was a girl who would grow to become a woman just like their own mothers. So I reminded them that when they called me names, they were calling their mother those names. This would make them back off a little because no one wanted their mothers insulted.

I am not sure where this fire came from. I guess partly it was the suppressed anger from watching my father beat up my mother on what felt like a daily basis, to living with a man who had sexually abused me, so I would fight back because I did not want another boy or man to cross my boundaries.

I remember the time my mother left me alone as she travelled to the United States, and I had to succumb to my father's verbal abuses night after night - I eventually fled from him. I ran away from home to live with my childhood best friend and her family for well over nine months. Again later, when I needed to get my scholarship in Zimbabwe to travel abroad for higher education, I fought all the way until I landed my dream school. I fought and argued against the denial of my Student Visa until they gave it to me. I had to flee and fight my way through everything.

The dichotomy of life

I love my father, and will always do. I miss him every day since his passing, but at the same time, I hated the man he was when he brutally beat my mother almost every night.

My father was the epitome of an amazing provider. He was a hardworking parent who deprived himself of luxurious materials to ensure we went to the best schools. I have many memories of my father and one of them was his entrepreneurial spirit. I remember him always having cash around the house, and I would always ask him for money for candy, or keep the change each time I went to buy his cigarettes and matches at the local tuck shop.

I remember sitting next to my dad as a young girl, volunteering to blow the match stick each time he would smoke. I would sit next to my father and always had so many inquisitive and sometimes silly questions, including how the men blowing the trumpet on the television breathed. He would tell me that they breathed both ways, which now as an adult, I realise was very humorous of my dad to say. I guess he had many of what they call "dad jokes" even though I didn't understand them at that young age.

My father gave me the best life lessons, though during that time, it was a bit irritating. Each term, before going back to boarding school, he would sit me down, and begin the same lecture, which I had memorized over the years.

It was his custom, then he would drive me off to the school bus with a lot more bags and trunks full of food to feed all my friends in my dorm.

I loved my father because I knew that he loved me a lot. At times, he seemed to have a strange way of showing it. He was not affectionate, but he showed in his actions and provision.

Growing up was always a confusing dichotomy. I lived in two worlds between my father who was a loving provider, and the man who always beat my mum - the woman I love, and also used derogatory words towards me.

I always went back and forth with this love-hate confusion. When I began healing as an adult, I actually had to take seven years of silence from my father, which was one of the hardest but needed seasons of my life.

I am thankful that before my father passed away, I had an opportunity to spend some quality time with him - just me and him and we talked about how I felt during my childhood.

My father never really apologized, and it was at that moment that I realized that he did the best he could with the strong patriarchal cultural environment and the information that was available to him. My father taught me to love deeper and forgive quickly because I always wondered what kind of war was happening within him. To use such violence on my mother on the one hand, but on the other, be tender and loving towards me as his daughter during the early years. I saw the best version of my dad, a well-meaning man who did have his demons but maybe did not realize it.

As a child, and even an adult now raising my children, I still do not fully understand how one person can be so loving and violent at the same time.

As a child you don't really understand what your parents have to go through to survive. So you accept dysfunction in whatever shades it comes in - it becomes the norm. Dysfunction came to our home in a hazy bottle of alcohol. The fiery liquid would turn the father that I loved into someone unrecognizable. We never knew who would walk into our home at the end of a hard day's work. Would it be the father that we loved and laughed with, or would it be the scary monster that sent us cowering?

Many nights when I heard my dad's car pull into the driveway, I would run fast to my bedroom and put a pillow on my head so that I didn't hear what would happen as he used his hands to beat my mother mercilessly. She tried to shelter us from the outrageous abuse, but there was nothing much that she could do. Our situation was so normal that the law enforcement officers expected us at the police station to report another charade, until they just got tired of responding. Yet in all the dysfunction this was our norm, filled with an ever-twisting vortex of love and despair.

In my case especially, already living with a physically and verbally abusive father, volumes could never describe living with multiple forms of abuse. My father was so erratic that I feared that even if I told my mother about the rape, he would blame me and then take it out on my mother for allowing her step-brother to enter our home.

This is why on the particular night that I was first raped, I had remembered happiness filling our home instead of havoc, because it was my "loving" father who had showed up in our home that night. Along with my mother and siblings, we were all having a good time. I always cherished those days when havoc was hidden. It was those times that allowed me to bond with my "true" parents in their state of existence outside of the challenges of life - one of the few times we had some happy laughter at night time in my home, and not my mother's usual screams for help, so I was relieved. Alas! Little did I know that my mother's loud screams would soon be replaced by my own silent screams - the silent screams that would haunt me for the rest of my adult life. I had to suffer in silence.

TAKE-AWAYS: Many young women who grow into mothers, elders and advisors, still need to heal wounds from broken relationships with their father figures, and any male figures that mattered in their childhood. This infected root needs to be uprooted because it causes a lot of trauma, which then bleeds into the present day.

The Tragic impacts of Trauma

I will now elaborate more on trauma and the effect that it has on us. This warrants a whole section because understanding and overcoming it is the key step to our healing and freedom. It may sound technical, however, stick with me, it will surely be worthwhile.

Knowledge is power and people perish because of lack of knowledge, therefore I have done all the research for you, so you don't have to.

So, What is trauma? Trauma is the process that one goes through after experiencing or witnessing something terrifying. It is an event that causes psychological, physical, emotional or mental harm through abuse, violence or even death. A traumatic event could also be called a loss event. If someone dies, that's a loss. If someone was abused, that too is a loss - a loss of trust. Whether you want to call the event trauma or a loss is ok, but the result of a traumatic event is GRIEF.

Grief is the normal and natural response to loss - the feelings one experiences after trauma, filled with conflicting emotions that result in the end of or change in a familiar pattern or behavior. Grief is the feeling of wishing things would have ended differently or better.

After doing my research, I have come to understand that there are six distinct types of trauma that you should know about most of which I have experienced.

1. Physical trauma- This is a serious and critical bodily injury, or shock from an external source eg domestic violence, beatings, torture, sexual violation.

2. Psychological trauma – Any critical incidents causing a person to experience strong emotional reactions that have the potential to affect the ability to function at work, home, with family or in other areas of their lives.

3. Social trauma – Any social condition that perpetuates forms of oppression against vulnerable populations e.g. war, hate crimes, poverty, homelessness, physical and verbal violence and addictions.

4. Historical trauma – Cross generational events of oppression, for example - massacre of American Indians, slavery of African Americans, Holocaust targeting Jewish people, and huge crimes against LGBT community.

5. Ongoing trauma – Not a single event. Continuous day to day for example - extreme poverty, chronic illness, addiction and all forms of prejudice and domestic violence abuse.

6. Vicarious trauma – Secondary traumatic distress experienced by the helpers e.g. family, friends, professionals, as a result of the empathy while assisting and caring for survivors of trauma. I experienced vicarious trauma as I watched my father abuse my mother constantly.

Trauma is not easy to work with and I cannot emphasise enough the importance of self-care and some form of therapy either professionally, or talking it out with someone who can listen and help.

Signs and symptoms of trauma:

It is important to be aware of these, especially for parents of young children.

Young children

Anxiety, bedwetting, temper tantrums, infantilism.

Girls

Withdrawal, anxiety, depression, self harming, eating disorders

Boys

Aggression, disobedience, copying violent behaviour, truancy, using alcohol and or drugs to cope with trauma

Both boys and girls

Poor school performance, post-traumatic stress disorder, flashbacks, nightmares, copied behaviours.

Trauma overrides normal adaptive functions, leaving the victim helpless and terrified in a world that feels out of control and unsafe. It has effects on our brains and bodies.

Impact on memory and emotions:

- It is possible to have no memory of the traumatic event but experience intense emotion or recall the event with no emotion.

- Protective shell dissociation – This can be conscious or unconscious, where alters are created. Feelings of hurt, fear or shame are avoided, and rage and anger are suppressed.

- Hypervigilance - there is a perpetual scanning of the environment to search for sights, sounds, people, behaviors, smells, or anything else that is reminiscent of activity, threat or trauma. The victim is placed on high alert in order to be certain that danger is not near. Hypervigilance can lead to a variety of obsessive behavior patterns, as well as producing difficulties with social interaction and relationships.

- Cortical process in brain breakdown during trauma is equal to memory not stored properly, painful memories stored as sensory fragments instead, persisting nightmares and flashbacks, forgotten landmines. Ref: Seigel (2001)

Links between childhood abuse and later life problems:

Remember there is evidence of links between childhood abuse and trauma and later life problems. This evidence is universal therefore it is not unique to people of any one race, colour, creed, religion or sexual orientation.

What can we do?

- Promote wellness

- Apply safeguarding principles in your own home

- Stop intergenerational trauma

- See something, say something

- Advocate for victims

- Provide a safe space for victims to talk

- Initiate and drive support programs

- Be your sister and your brother's keeper

Cultural Toxicity

I recall always fighting against the idea of going to the butchery over the school holidays and no one seemed to notice this strange retaliation. They probably assumed I was just being rebellious. I was avoiding having to constantly be in the same environment as my abuser - my step uncle who worked for my father there. This is another lesson to parents. Pay attention to your children when they seem to feel uncomfortable towards an individual or attending certain events or doing certain tasks with people. Always ask open ended questions and allow your children to be comfortable enough to share more in depth about their discomfort.

If we are too busy or oblivious as parents, we tend to miss these signs. This is why I have dedicated 'family meeting times' with my children. This we do as a tradition without any television, games or distractions. We simply have a meal together and talk about all issues that come to mind. I try to create a space for them to share more things with me, in a place where they feel safe.

It is important to note that the people who sexually abuse our children are often people close to us - those people who know the child very well, as in the case of my step-uncle. It was right there, under the same roof as my parents and siblings. While everyone was still in high spirits, watching the new first ever color television in my neighborhood, my rapist took the opportunity to perform this cruel, psychopathic and evil act. He took advantage of all the excitement and emotional climate that everyone was experiencing that night, so that it would have been easy to dismiss claims of violation if I were ever brave enough to tell anyone. It would have also been easy for anyone to want to blame me for shutting down the happiness and jubilation that we had all experienced as a result of the new TV.

This typical calculated move is something that parents must always keep track of. Make sure you look beyond what you see. Look closer when you have other people around your children. I am not encouraging you to become paranoid, however be vigilant.

I also want to encourage parents to be always aware, as the people who molest young children know how to be close to the children and family. They are often in close proximity, or will find ways to get close to your child.

It was during those moments when my mother asked me to go to bed and rest for the next day of school, that a child molester calculated his move. He knew our home routine and was familiar with everyone's habits. It is at this time that I want to urge parents and guardians to always be on guard and watch closely, the people around your children.

Some people say, "Why didn't you tell someone?" Well, sexual abuse is as much mental trauma as it is physical. Your life balance is blown to bits, especially as a young innocent child. How can a young child figure out how to deal with this predicament at that tender age? It's hard enough for a fully developed and functional adult... let alone a child! With no emotional intelligence or articulation, constant threats over their heads and a culture that places importance on masculinity and positional authority - children are taught to obey whatever their elders command, so at the time it seemed there was no way out. I really had no voice.

Growing up in an African household, I remember hearing statements from parents like " I am not your friend, but your parent", or "I will kill you and return you where you came from, if you talk back to me". Though they didn't mean the literal 'killing', it was enough to instill fear in you to stop doing or saying what was considered offensive and disrespectful to them. It was commonplace in many households, whereby such statements were used to strike a balance of the respect that parents and any elders were to earn from children.

As I mentioned earlier, being in a highly patriarchal society with objectification of the girl child, it was not only typical in some families for men to also use derogatory terms on their wives and daughters in the home, but also outside the home to random women and even co-workers. It was considered normal and even acceptable, especially back then. Men felt like they had the right to say and do anything they wanted to any woman or girl - typical toxic masculinity fuelled by cultural rules that they had created. It's only in recent years that the women empowerment movement has brought about some change in perception and behaviours from men. We still have a long way to go, however I acknowledge how far we have come. Women empowerment does not mean the emasculation of men - it simply means that both male and female genders are of equal value and deserve the same respect as human beings.

The name calling from both my father and random male figures around me, was something that affected and eventually seared my conscience. As I got a little older, my father would tell me in his drunken state that I would just become a prostitute like all the other girls and would never amount to anything. All this cultural toxicity created a harsh environment where women and girls were constantly violated without any defense.

In light of this however, I want to invite you if you are a parent and or future parent, to pause and reflect on how you were parented or how you may be parenting your children. Think about how this may impact the ability of your children to feel comfortable to share any abuse that may be happening or happened to them. Think about how your words create part of their childhood identity, that some are never able to grow out of.

We must challenge our parenting styles because growing up, my culture and the traditional African parenting that my folks implemented included the notion that a child ought to be seen and not heard. You could not speak up your opinions. It's easy to imagine that in such an environment, a child would certainly not feel empowered to speak up. I urge all parents reading this book to self-reflect on an empowering parenting style - one that fosters a two-way respectful relationship between your children and yourself - one that encourages trust, and does not stifle their little voices.

CHAPTER 3

FROM POT TO FIRE

Grown-ish

I always love the rain, because it reminds me of a lot of the joyous moments from my childhood, especially its ability to block me from hearing loud noises of my mother crying or the thumping of her head against the wall next to my bedroom.

The rain is also what helped me that early morning when I decided to run away from home at age sixteen, after my mother travelled to the United States to visit my eldest sister, leaving me with my father and the maid whom I felt like I took care of most of the time. That is another conversation.

Unlike most girls my age, I never had a normal childhood. I always sensed this because when you are in boarding school, you get to spend more time with your school mates, than you do with your siblings at home. This is where you discover how normal or dysfunctional your growing up is.

There was a raging warfare within me, torn between the relief of being away from home and the utter fear that I would hear of my mother's death any day, from my father's beating. These issues at home affected how I showed up in my adolescent days. I learned from an early age how to compartmentalize and also how to show people what they needed to see and hide what I needed to hide.

I have often heard people say, let children be children and play - this is their primary role at this stage. Well I never had that or learned how to play. I often hear that I need to take myself less seriously and play more. Well this is something I was not familiar with - certainly not after all the trauma I had already endured.

Throughout my high school I would carefully pick my friends, and developed a deeper spiritual practice because it was in this that I found peace and safety. I also learned not to have too many friends or open up to friends because I needed to ensure that not many people knew about my home life. This quality would impact my ability to make and keep friendships which later showed up in my adult life.

When I think about the last twenty years of my life, I realize that I have been running away from my own shadow. After experiencing my father's endless nights of yelling and cursing me out, I realised that I had become my mother's replacement for the first four months that she travelled to the United States to help my older sister with her newborn baby.

Night after night my father would come home after midnight. He would wake me up and ask me to listen to him. Most times the conversation would begin with a lecture that would turn into insults.

I realized the dichotomy that my father existed in - the loving nurturing father who wanted good things for me and hence the constant lectures. Then the drunk man who would turn into a monster I couldn't recognise! One night, I had enough and so I left my parent's house and rana away.

From my teenage years until my early thirties, I had been running away from pain and anything that represented itself as danger in my sight. I mastered this survival technique of running away and it manifested as instability and short-term shallow relationships over and over again.

When I think about my childhood into my adolescent years, the time I moved away from Zimbabwe to the United States to study, I describe this period as my "Valley and dark moments". It was a time I did not realize I had wounds and what happens when you do not tend to a wound is that it grows deeper and infection takes place. Also, when you are navigating a Valley without a campus, it is easy to go in circles and miss the way to the top of the Mountain.

I would spend my adolescent years running away. First, I ran away from home because I thought this would give me the peace I was looking for. The trend continued after living with my best friend's family for almost a year, where I then successfully ran away furthest north, moving to Minnesota USA.

I had failed to realize that all-important saying ... 'Wherever you go, there you are'.

Wherever I was going to go, I was always going to find myself and as long as I ran away from my pain, by changing my physical location, I would still show up with my wounds, deeper and more infected each time.

As I ran, this became a skill I was very good at and it would take me another decade and a stretch of running from the pot into the fire, where I would engage in new relationships with the bleeding wounds. I went from one valley into the next, only to find that it was lower, deeper and darker than the last.

In retrospect I was carrying infected wounds I was not aware I had. It was the foul smell of an infection that was very much invisible, but showed up in the quality of life I lived. These symptoms showed up in the kind of men and friendships I attracted.

Thank goodness my infections did not become septic to my death, but I did bleed onto others. I could not keep friendships, and those good nurturing friends I had, I could not maintain or give emotion to. I remember one particular friend of mine reaching out to tell me that she was getting married one Spring. I was excited and filled with emotion, mostly of happiness for her, but also shame for myself.

I had let my friend down because I was sleepwalking through my life with my infections. I could not be the friend she was to me or she needed me to be, and yet she had the decency to reach out to me and inform me of her wedding.

Moments of reflection with one of my best friends have enabled me to appreciate the accountability and ownership of my predicaments. I realise that I cannot just blame the Valley moments to those who came into my life and abused me. The first step of healing for me was acknowledging that indeed I had deep wounds, infected smelling wounds, that were bleeding over in spaces I showed up.

I had to address each site of my infection without overlooking the harm done to me by others, but the ability to hold my contribution in one hand, and in the other hand, their own contributions.

It would create vicious cycles of what felt like dejavu to me. I would meet the same kind of people, and duplicate unhealthy relationships until that moment when I opened my eyes. I had finally located my source of infection.

When you are in the Valley, there are always some choices to make: Either find a way back to the Mountaintop, or let the vultures and the valley swallow you.

I could not afford to die in the valley so I invested my energy and time in understanding, preparing, studying and gathering tools of knowledge. It would later support me and give me direction on my way back to the top.

As I think about the wound analogy, it also parallels a tooth infection. At times you may experience some sensitivity on your tooth. Maybe it hurts at times when you brush it or when it comes in contact with hot or cold water. Only when you go to the dentist, when they can actually take some X Rays, is when you determine that the tooth is infected and the level of decay. Your dentist then determines the treatment plan after the examinations are carried out.

With this in mind, one of the main questions I want to leave you my dear reader, is to examine honestly those areas of your life that you need to revisit. Push yourself to be honest and accountable, so you can begin to heal.

If you don't realize that you are living in a Valley, or what I call the lowest version of yourself, there is no creative energy there, nor abundance. You are unable to change if you are not aware that there are underlying causes to your issues in life. This space represents negative things, like the Sheol, lifelessness and lack. Once you identify the space you are in, then you can begin to create ways to climb out of it.

Issues in my tissues

I am going to share more personal stories and experiences with you. Those that I call issues in my tissues. Some people may think it is too revealing, but I think it is important not to give you fluff. My goal is to be authentic and transparent with you if it will save your life.

I had to let go of my first love who intended to marry me, because of the long distance with my plans to study abroad whilst he resided in Zimbabwe. This made it especially difficult and challenging. He had paid the bride price for me, and as our tradition requires, my family tried to return his dowry. My ex-estranged husband became bitter, to the point of punishing not only myself, but my whole family. Having another man pay dowry and still refusing it back, keeps a leash on you according to my tradition. Just recently again, his parents contacted my sister and said that they would now like me to send them some money so they can set me free. As a daughter of Africa, I believe that in this moment, I began to connect the dots of why my romantic relationships have failed dismally. I have since been engaged over three times and in each case, the men just wander away.

What is interesting about this situation is that he has moved on. He is married, with three children and I remain somehow a prisoner of a traditional dowry that was paid for me over 20 years ago, and never lived with this man.

Anyhow, when I moved to the United States, I met a partner. From my experience when I got pregnant with his child, my first born, he was not ready to raise a family and asked me to have an abortion, which I refused. That was when the torture began.

As a new immigrant who was unable to work legally and being pregnant, my partner began to punish me by withholding food and basic needs from me.

I remember going hungry while pregnant, having cravings and not being able to get the food I craved for and also feeling embarrassed and alone. I was desperate and managed to get a job where I was taking care of a friend's grandmother, who was in hospice care. I would work overnight, which was difficult for me being newly pregnant and very sick, but this job was my saving grace - it allowed me to have enough money to buy a few clothes for my unborn baby.

This was a moment when I was living in my pain, coupled with childhood trauma, that I was unaware of. I had issues hidden in my tissues. I found myself in the exact same environment as in my childhood. The same environment I had fought so hard to run away from when I left my home country of Zimbabwe at the tender age of seventeen.

Again, I clearly remember at St Paul Minnesota - The Capital Court House, with my young friend, who would soon become my son's godmother. There I was, seven months pregnant and my then boyfriend leaned in, looked at me and whispered, "I am just doing this to help you with your immigration situation".

I will never forget this day, nor those chilling words.

Rejection took a deeper root, and I would spend all my twenties, into early thirties missing it as my primary cause of infection in my romantic relationships.

After my first child was born, I decided to run again from this arrangement that was loveless and a pity move from the man who made me pregnant. As my son got older, my partner started entertaining the idea of revisiting the drawing board and actually renewing the vows to become a family again. However, he had crossed the line of hurting me, fuelled by his unfaithfulness, coupled with emotional and physical abuse.

So I refused.

Upon meeting the father of my next babies, my twins, I tried again to establish some stability and build a family. His marriage proposal was very welcome as we both wanted this stability. Considering my divorce after fourteen years of previous marriage and a history of infertility, the twins seemed like the miracle and glue that would keep us together, but alas in due time, we would go our separate ways.

I had attracted a worse version of my ex-husband who was very toxic.

I remember on one occasion, as caring for three toddlers under the age of five, had taken a toll on my health. Unlike being back in my home country of Zimbabwe, when a woman gives birth, she is often sent to her mother's home to get support. In my culture, there is a six-week period one must spend, where she is catered to and her primary job is to nurse her newborn, and the whole family supports her.

I believe these and other traditional practices have kept women in my culture free of diseases like postpartum depression. The opposite was my experience after I had my twin babies. Not only was I alone, but I was in a strange culture.

That particular day, my partner and I were arguing because his mother was on her way to pick him up and "give him a break", leaving me alone for an unknown period of time with the twins who were barely two weeks old. I also had my three and a half year old son from my previous marriage with me.

Standing on the stair care, while holding my two week old baby girl, I tried to negotiate with my partner, and pleaded with him to not leave me. My body was tired, and I needed him to just stay and help me with the children, especially my three year old son.

I am not sure, I recall what happened, but the next thing I remember was that I was at the bottom of the staircase. Holding my baby tight and in a panic, I took my cell phone and called the local police.

I had just experienced physical abuse while carrying my child. My head was hit hard on the concrete floor, and my body served as a shield for my daughter. I would later get assistance from some young mentees of mine, who allowed me to move in with them. With three children and a suitcase, I began a journey to freedom from an abusive relationship.

It took me over ten years to finally establish a safe living environment after this incident, but I did it. When a partner puts their hands on you, this is Domestic violence and is something that should not be excused or tolerated. Whenever someone intentionally hurts you, it means that love is no longer being served. It is time to collect your dignity and crown dear Queen, and move on.

Indeed, when I look at my first ten years in the United States, it was a valley that contained in it a rock bottom as well.

The beauty about being at rock bottom is that there is nowhere else to go but back up. As a believer I also know that Jesus Christ is the Rock of all ages, so in those rock bottom moments, he was the foundation I had to stay in.

I know it can be difficult to leave for various reasons. Some women are attached to status or material belongings, whilst others stay for their children, and still, others stay in hopes that their abusive partner will change. As research records, it can take up to seven times for a woman to finally leave an abusive relationship. It is unfortunate because in this seven times statistic, many women lose their lives to domestic homicide.

At the beginning of April in Minnesota alone for example, we had ten women who were killed due to domestic violence. These are only recorded numbers, how much more are those unrecorded?

Sizing Up

As life progressed, I decided to seek counsel from a Therapist. During my first coaching and healing session, she would lead me into meditation where she asked me to close my eyes, and revisit my twenty five-year old pregnant younger self. Initially, I fought it, then finally yielded.

To my shock, the physical reaction to this exercise would cause me less resistance, as I realized one of the main wounds I was avoiding. I had a wake-up call that I was harbouring so much ANGER. That was the emotion that came up when we went deeper into meditation - the anger of rejection, as I replayed the scenario in my head. It was an anger I would internalize and it would cause yet another wound site in my soul, showing up in a series of unhealthy relationships, both platonic and romantic.

Six years after my divorce from my abusive ex, I found myself at the onset of another abusive relationship. I was now wiser, having attended therapy. On the second day in New York City, where I had gone to visit this man that a friend of mine connected me to, I had just finished explaining to him about my personality type. This in my understanding is Type A or Alpha female. I proudly described how I was a champion for women, and in essence, tried to gain his validation of the journey I had travelled up to this moment.

To my amazement, this man went on a rampage for what seemed like an eternity, in very condescending and demeaning words. He tore apart each part of my narrative about myself, leaving me in utter shock! I had just attracted my ex-husband, if not worse.

Of course, it would have been the first and last trip to New York with this man, as well as the end of that relationship. I responded to him, calmly using the tools in my toolbox, from the women's healing circle I had attended five years prior. Letting my new and soon to be ex boyfriend know that I would never again tolerate any other man or woman negating who I am, I would speak my truth. It was his right to disagree, but disagree, respectfully. I walked away, with grace, and never contacted this man again. I had just won, I had just survived, and taught another person how to treat me.

After this experience, the first serious relationship I had post divorce, was to a wonderful and also very wealthy and powerful man. At first I did not realize that almost everyone around him was benefiting something from him, because I was in my own path of financial success. I was not looking at him in that manner. However, over time, I realized that I had fallen victim to a lot of his friends and family because they would create situations to make me react with anger, and feel insecure about whether or not I should trust my boyfriend.

I remember a sister of his bringing some female friends to her birthday party, and in some ways, trying to introduce one of the ladies to my boyfriend so she could have him. To this I reacted with anger, only to become the center of attention that night and labeled angry. Another incident was always with his staff member, the man I once caught going through my purse. He and his wife always seemed to plant seeds of doubt by mentioning vague statements, like "keep your eyes open", and "you never know what people are up to." This left me so confused and paranoid, with more questions.

Finally, I managed to speak to my mentor about these incidents. She is one of the wisest women I am blessed to call a second mother, and she made me realize that those people around my boyfriend were after benefiting from him. I had become a threat to those benefits. As our relationship grew stronger and more serious, his focus would shift to settling down to have a family, and of course, with a strong assertive African queen by his side, I would protect my family's interests therefore I was a threat to them victimizing my boyfriend.

My mentor helped me realize that in fact, I had fallen prey to being victim to those folks around the man I fell in love with. I share this story to teach you a skill I got from my mentor - How to size up your life situations. Sizing up any potentially victimizing situation before you decide what to do about it, is crucial to avoid becoming a victim. Whenever you are about to enter into a social interaction, you must have your eyes wide open, so you can avoid being done even before the possible drama of victimization has begun to unfold on you.

Today in my work, I hear a lot of stories about women being abused, not just by their intimate partner, but most times, the rest of the partner's family as well. I recall a few cases of women, whose mother in law, and sister in laws, partook in the abuse more than the husband who was also abusive to her. This is utterly appalling, so it is critical to size up your life situations, open your eyes, think ahead, and always be prepared before it unfolds on you.

As I write this, I do not want you to feel that you have to reach some level of paranoia, where you assume that everyone around you has ill intentions. Of Course this would not be a healthy way to live, nor would it be a freedom fulfilled life either.

Sizing up your life situation means being alert and developing a new kind of intelligence which just naturally keeps you from being abused. It means assessing the needs of people who you will be dealing with and anticipating what course of action would be best for you in attaining your own objectives. You want to be getting along with people who are willing to respect where you stand. Sizing up your life is crucial if you are to avoid circumstances which trap you into self-forfeiting actions.

I learnt how to guard my heart as the book of Proverbs asserts, 'From the heart, the issues of life flow'. If I did not find ways to guard my heart, compartmentalize my pain and make a solid plan to deal with it, I would lose my mind. In a lot of ways, it was me against the world.

In a world that thrives so well on controlling and regulating you, you must often be 'unreasonable or insubordinate', to people who would manipulate you. If you do not take this power position, you will otherwise fall prey to being victimized. In my short time on this earth I have come to a realization that the world is full of people who would love you to behave in whatever ways are most convenient for them.

I have many examples of how to teach people how to treat you. If you would like to be completely in charge of your life, despite domestic violence, or cultural enslavement by other people's beliefs, you need to get to a point where you will not automatically do things according to other people's plans.

To live your life the way you choose, you have to be a bit rebellious. You have to be willing to stand up for yourself. You might have to appear a bit disturbing to those who have strong interests in controlling your behavior, but being your own person is a worthy cause that will absolutely enhance your life.

To achieve this level of freedom, you will have to be an ordinary human being, who simply says to the world and everyone in it, "I am going to be my own person, and resist anyone who tries to stop me".

Victim or Victor

Let's talk a bit more about Domestic Violence.

The term Domestic Violence and abuse is used to describe any incident or pattern of incidence of controlling and threatening behaviour, violence or abuse between people who are intimately involved or from a family member.

These incidents may be physical, sexual, financial or emotional, including verbal threats and controlling behaviour. Violence and forced marriages are forms of domestic violence and abuse.

Nowadays Domestic abuse can also happen on mobile phones, on the Internet and on social networking sites in other words it just doesn't happen at home.

According to the American Journal of Emergency Medicine, statistics since the beginning of the pandemic indicate that in November 2020, increase in police recorded data for offences flagged a high domestic violence abuse rate, exacerbated by the coronavirus pandemic and lockdown.

Improved police recording put a question on whether it can be determined if this increase was directly attributed to the coronavirus pandemic, however police service received an increased number of calls for domestic incidents following the lockdown, largely driven by third-party calls.

There was generally an increase in demand for domestic abuse victims services during the pandemic which indicated an increase in the severity of abuse being experienced and a lack of available coping Mechanisms such as the ability to leave the home.

52% felt that the pandemic had a bad effect on their mental health and that they were less able to cope with the abuse.

91% say the pandemic has impacted the experience of abuse in one or more ways.

58% say they felt they had no one to turn to for help.

52% felt more afraid.

51% reported that the violence and abuse had gotten worse.

53% reported that the children had witnessed more abuse towards them.

50% were scared that the children would be left alone with the abuser.

There are Lack of incorporating statistics specific to asylum seekers immigrants in the poor communities.

I shared these statistics with you to understand the severity of this greater global pandemic known as Domestic violence that has killed countless victims since the beginning of time.

Anytime you find yourself controlled by someone else, out of control of your life, you are being victimized. The key word is CONTROL. If you are not in the driver's seat of your life or making the key decisions, then you are being manipulated by someone.

A victim is described as someone who is taken advantage of. You can be robbed or swindled in much more damaging ways when you give up your emotional and behavioral control in the course of everyday life. Victims are people who run their lives according to the dictates of others. You find yourself doing things you would really rather not do, or being manipulated into activities loaded with unnecessary personal sacrifice that breed hidden resentment. To be victimized, as I use the word here means to be governed and checked by forces outside yourself and while those forces are unquestionably ubiquitous. In our modern day times, you can rarely be victimized unless you allow it to happen.

People also victimize themselves in numerous ways throughout the everyday business of life. From things like not knowing how to set boundaries, to overworking oneself, people-pleasing, keeping up with the Joneses, not forgiving yourself, the list goes on as we will reveal in the following chapters.

Victims almost always operate from weakness. They let themselves be dominated and pushed around because they often feel they are not smart enough or strong enough to be in charge of their lives. So they hand the keys of their lives to the other person, get off the driver's seat and become a passenger in their own vehicle.

If you are behaving in self-defeating ways, miserable, hurt, anxious, afraid to be yourself, or feel immobilized, then you are a victim. I know the question of religion and God will come into play here. Religious institutions have become increasingly a place of victimizing people. I always say be very careful of any religious leader that assumes that only they can hear from God. This has become another pandemic across the Globe, with many falling prey to victimization.

God is in control of the universe, but He is a just God who has given mankind free will. He even states in the Bible that He has given each one of us a purpose and gift that we must freely use. God has grace and mercy, therefore giving up your will power to God is not becoming a victim. When I talk about manipulation and control, I am referring to man-made institutions from one human being to another - not God.

The question should be, how does one get freedom from being a victim - will you be a victim or a victor?

My love of world history has taught me that no one has obtained freedom for free, nor is it handed on a silver platter. Wars have been fought to obtain freedom, and if someone hands freedom to you freely, then it is not real freedom. Freedom means you are unobstructed in ruling your own life as you please. It is when you recognize that anything short of your expectations is not good enough, and you unapologetically let the world know.

The right to live your life outside of what others want you to be is freedom. Most people will try to label your push for freedom as 'selfish' and will really be protesting your threats to being free from their victimization. They will try to make you feel guilty as they try to immobilize you again.

Growing up in an African household as the last born, I can clearly recall some of my siblings, trying to tell me what major I ought to pursue in University. This was often because it was what was familiar to them and their fields, but I had my own unique vision that God gave me. Culturally you are obligated to listen and follow what your elders or older siblings tell you to do. However, from a young age I learned to be assertive about my choices - following my intuitive voice, rather than the external pushes from family.

Working extensively in women's mental health institutions and through healing women, I realized that the first and most undermined source of victimization is family. I love my family so much, in fact, I believe that my family is the reason I am the woman I am today, but what many people will not say is that most people are victimized in family first. From being told how to be, how and who to worship, how to dress, some of these familial values, and cultural norms, tend to cross over to victimize family members, as they later on try to figure their own individual paths in life.

To be free does not mean denying your responsibilities to your loved ones and your fellow man. Indeed, it includes the freedom to make choices, to be responsible. However, nowhere is it dictated that you must be what others want you to be when their wishes conflict with what you want for yourself. You can be responsible and free.

I cannot emphasize enough that growing up in an African household, you were often victimized simply by virtue of your status, as a child in the family, or student in the school. You were to be seen and not heard. Talking back or voicing your opinion to your parents, would be punishable by a very long whipping and also oftentimes, asked not to make a crying sound despite the pain from the whip. You never had the keys nor access to the driver's seat - you would just complain under your breath in private and could not show your emotions, disappointment or anger towards adults.

I am not sure about other cultures, but as I am raising second generation Zimbabwean-American children, sometimes, I have to catch my breath, as my eight year old twins, and eleven year old son, voice their opinions, and at times vocally disagree with my decisions for them.I realize in my parenting journey that in fact, I have been carrying many left - over habits from childhood that made some practical sense but set me up to inhibit my children from practising their freedom.

As an adult, I also realize that I have had to undo and unlearn a lot from my childhood, which has set me up to be an easy victim for others as well. Getting out of your victim traps involves, above all, developing new habits. Healthy habits are learned in the same way as those unhealthy habits through practice, after you become aware of what you are going to practice. Victim or victor - the choice is yours.

CHAPTER 4

BORN A CRIME

The Criminal Justice System

We will discuss more about the different types of abuses in later chapters. For now, I would like to focus on what is known as 'Divorce Court Abuse'.

The players in the scenario include a Black African immigrant woman, who has decided to file for divorce. The abuser and perpetrator is a white man, typically more financially well off, and there are children involved. The judge is often an old white man.

When this scenario starts, generally the odds are often in the woman's favor. However, with the particular characters involved and based on racism and connections, this can quickly turn against her. This was my story, and sadly continues to play all over again for many women I work with. Unfair court systems that are rooted in systemic racism, and are not an equal playing field for Black women.

For six years after my divorce, I experienced continued abuse where my ex partner used the court systems to alienate me from my son. It would take that long for me to win the fight, as it was only when my child could essentially tell the judge in his own words that his father's new wife was abusing him and he felt safer in my care.

There is an invisible type of abuse that I would like to introduce to the world - Parental Alienation. If you want to kill a woman whilst she is alive, take her babies away from her. As one of my clients who was taken away from her mother at age five recalls, she saw her mother 'die' alive, whilst walking in that moment, because of parental alienation.

The foster care systems and court systems never serve black women or black mothers justly in the United States. The decision always comes down to the race and character of the Judge sitting on that throne of power. He is often an older White man, and if the abuser is also a White man, one must ask this: what is the bias to the judgement?

I believe that this subject matter needs to be addressed at length and I have started a Healing Group of Alienated mothers of color on social media because I realize how rampant the issue is.

Sadly this scenario keeps playing over and over again in my work and in many ways, it feels like a Dejavu. Nevertheless, my spirituality reminds me that this is how God uses pain, to propel you to purposeful service to others.

With an 'unjust' criminal justice system stacked against people of color, there is very little hope for us. It took the death of George Floyd in my state of Minnesota, and the global uproar, for some people to see this blatant and open racism that happens daily in our society. What is worse, is that women are not usually treated equally with respect. They are considered as second class citizens due to gender inequalities and toxic masculinity, leaving the black woman at the very bottom of the food chain - a concept that Kimberle Crenshaw coined as Intersectionality. In other words, before we even come into the presence of a judge, we are guilty before being proven innocent - we are 'born a crime' as Trevor Noah puts it. Intersectionality is the interconnected nature of social categorisations such as race, class, and gender, regarded as creating overlapping and interdependent systems of discrimination or disadvantage. This can be in any sphere or sector of life - whether it's socially, financially or politically, not just the criminal justice system.

A white man is at an advantage over a black man. A man is at an advantage over a woman. A white woman is at an advantage over a black woman, leaving the black woman at an intersection that leaves us the most disadvantaged.

The lack of financial access for women of color means they are not able to hire good attorneys, which in turn means they cannot have a good solid representation to fight for their children. It boils down to just that - a numbers game as well as who has access to who and what.

It is never about who is the healthier parent, and what enrages me is that the children are forgotten. Like my son, for six years he was exposed to abuse and at the age of 11, he was forced to fight for his freedom from abuse. This is heartbreaking and I am well aware that there is more of this happening than we can even fathom.

I am working on Legislation Change in Minnesota to ensure that less privileged women can have equal access to parenting time and that their networth does not equate to whether or not they are a good mother.

One important piece of information I want to share with you is, don't be emotional in court. I know it is a lot easier said than done, but you must go to each court hearing with a poker face. Don't allow your abuser or his attorney to see you showing any emotion. They are not your friends, advocates, or anyone who wants to support you by being fair. If you need to cry or be upset, wait until you get home or have access to a restroom!

Make sure you have an attorney that will fight for you and has the best interest for you and your child/ren. It is very important to hire an attorney that is familiar with domestic violence and the characteristics of abusers. If not, your attorney may be manipulated by your abuser. Your local women's shelter may be able to provide you with a list of local attorneys that are familiar with working on divorce cases that involve domestic violence and narcissistic abuse. Also, ensure that you never allow anyone to define your experience. You are the only one who has walked in your shoes, so do not be manipulated into trivialising your experiences.

Me against the world

My son sleeps with me at 11 years old. He refuses to sleep in his bedroom, so he lies next to me every night, and we watch Bible stories and talk about what we learned. It's only been three months since I have slept under the same roof with my baby in the last five years. I feel like in some way, this is my way of making up for lost time.

Just as we were starting to form a routine, another curve ball was thrown. It was a normal day, and I could hear the birds chirping on a peaceful Saturday morning. Out of my usual routine that particular morning, I just decided at the last minute, I wasn't going to the gym. Normally, my oldest son enables me to afford this 'me time' as he does his homework online while I leave him with his siblings for at least an hour to exercise, and then return to get ready for our day. As a protective mother, I try not to overdo it, so I skip my gym sessions sometimes and do home based workouts instead. Sometimes, I just do not have the extra time so I manage my day around the children.

That particular morning however, I had the time, but my Spirit refused to go to the gym, and my intuition whispered to me to stay home and stay put. So I did, and soon enough, I would learn why this message to be home that morning came to me. Looking through the closed blinds from our sun room, my daughter screamed, "They are here! I think it is Tyler's dad, grandpa and some strange man".

Three men showed up at my doorstep! It was my ex-husband, his father and their friend. I got a strange feeling because this same scenario played out when my oldest son was only six years old. They had previously taken my son away from me, in Iowa, where I had found my first stable job. My ex husband, who is also my abuser, had agreed verbally that I take my son with me to Iowa. He himself was mentally stressed due to some changes in his own life, but it seems that his parents always have a way of influencing how he takes his next steps.

Prior to this, my son had been taken away from me and I had to beg my ex husband to see him all that time. My son complained about the abuse that was happening in his father's house as he had brought in a new woman from Liberia who had a daughter that was two years older than him.

My heart sank. I was not about to have another nightmare Déjàvu. You see, exactly five years before, on a highway in the neighboring State of Iowa, these same men had called the police on me, ambushed and literally yanked my son out of my car. To add insult to injury, they filed charges that I had stolen my son across state lines.

How could I have abducted my own child, when during that time, I was living with my ex husband. He had made me rent out his basement with all my three children.

I had gotten my first job to work for the State Department in Iowa, and I had asked my ex husband if I could take my son so I could try and rebuild my life to get out of this rut of being homeless, and he had agreed.

I was right in the middle of my career taking an upward movement at the height of it, including the opportunity to work with Hillary Clinton's Campaign where I was nominated the first black Democratic representative from Iowa.

Yet again, there I was, back to the place I had been trying to get away from…. downhill again. I said to myself… "Not this time!!!" I was not going to let them take me back there. Not in 2021! I was not going to let anyone pull my strings.

I was not a victim anymore but a victor. I held the space with power and invited support immediately.

I decided that, since they used the police before to take my child away, I was going to use the police to keep my son. So I called my local police officers and six cop cars showed up in this very quiet cul de sac, expensive neighborhood that I finally acquired for a quieter life.

I hated the moment I called the police. You see, living in the suburbs as a black woman is rare especially during this time of racial tensions and heightened sensitivity. I have valued serenity, peace and privacy, as I don't want to be seen much. I don't want my blackness to be conspicuous in my neighbourhood, so this was one of those things that just brought a lot of attention to my home and the kids.

When the cops showed up, they came into my home and tried to make me feel comfortable, but as an African immigrant woman, I will never be comfortable with the police in my veins. I felt like I was carrying the weight of the whole world on my shoulders. It was me against the world. They interviewed my son, and to their amazement, my son strongly in his very quiet, shy, shaky voice told them he did not want to go to his father's house, because he does not feel safe there. He wanted to stay with his mommy and he was not going to go.

In fact, he told the police that he didn't want to go back to school in person. He was going to try and do his school online, because if he went back to school in person, his father would take him from the school and not return him home to us.

The officers went outside. I'm not sure what they were talking about for what seemed like the longest four minutes of my life! They came back with a decision. Ma'am, we cannot take your child out of your home. My whole body lost it. I lost it. I just grabbed my son, embraced him and started to cry.

It was a cry of both release and reminder of what happened six years ago. I was beginning to finally have some breakthrough with my son.

The cycle continues

I had begun to notice a pattern. Since our marriage failed, and even before then, once my ex husband's family got involved, for some reason he lost control.

But that morning, I wasn't going to let that cycle repeat itself. I was going to fight for my son and instead, it turns out that he helped me do that at his tender age of 11.

There is a reason it is called a Cycle of Abuse. There is always a pattern with abusive partners, or former partners. A continuous vicious cycle of finding ways to maintain Power and Control. In my case, like many, they use the Courts systems to do so. They kept my children's passports away from me and cut my ability to introduce my children to my African family members and or travel with them. This had been hindering my access to participate in the children's school activities in various states, and was used as a weapon for them to control and retain power.

I now have my son with me and have been hiring lawyers to win back his custody - an adversity and pain I had never anticipated in my life.

Today, I am happy to report that I got my children's passports and was able to take them on an unforgettable trip of a lifetime to Africa, where they thoroughly enjoyed themselves and got connected to their roots.

One may be wondering how many more women are going through this.

In my experience, the more I started standing up and raising eyebrows, the more women showed up in my workplace. For many migrant women who might want to speak up as well, the language barrier of not being able to speak English and lack of education about the system becomes a hindrance that puts them at a disadvantage. They go through this a lot and end up losing their children to the system, because typically the man who abuses them uses the children as a leverage of power and control. This Parental Alienation is a form of abuse that people don't talk about often enough.

The abuser paints the other parents as unstable, normally due to financial incapabilities. The child has no say, when they are too young.

You see, my son from the age of six had been trying to tell his dad that his wife and her sister were abusive towards him and he was not comfortable in his house because of this. However, to my amazement, my ex husband didn't seem to care or hear or see his own child. It took him five years, after numerous therapy sessions and mediation for him to finally realise this. Through my son's ability to code and create animations to tell and communicate to his dad what was happening to him, it took him five years to hear his child. It took him that fateful day when my son blatantly refused to go back home with his father. That's how much it took.

All this experience has made me extremely anxious. In fact, my son has been observing me. My body wakes up at 3:30am and I jump out of bed. My heart races. Every morning, I have to perform a ritual to calm down from panic attacks.

My heart will be beating so fast, I have nightmares that they would have taken my children. They say that to kill a mother slowly is to take her babies away from her whilst she is still alive. This is another reason why many women stay in abusive relationships for the sake of the children. They cannot bear a life without them in the case of their partner winning custody against them.

People often judge and make assumptions, but only the owner knows where the shoe pinches.

One woman once asked me out of spite. I don't think it was really from a place of love but she asked me, 'So, what do you do with your kids when you're doing all this traveling?' You see, I took on a hobby of travel because I realised that if you physically take me away from the place that gives me so much pain, it helps me to cope better. After all, this is why most people travel and go on holidays right? It is to escape the realities of life and take a break.

Traveling, going to speak to various groups, conferences and empowering other women were my coping skills to deal with being away from my children when they were in their father's custody.

Some women comment on how they could never let another woman take charge of their children, or they could not leave sight of their babies. I often chuckle because I understand that as long as you have not had to deal with these painful situations, you will always make those assumptions. What this part of my pain or adversity taught me is the importance of compartmentalizing pain - in a way, building a strategy on how you respond to situations in a manner that preserves your own mental health.

With this cycle, I realized that I could just settle or keep fighting with everything I had. I had fought myself to bankruptcy. I had fought with all my savings. I fought for my children to homelessness. I fought with everything I had until I realized that, in addition to the homelessness and an empty savings bank account, I was going to have an empty mind.

I was going to go insane and lose my mind, so I decided to preserve my mind. I started to work on my life and rebuild myself financially, so that I could position myself and leverage my power to fight back.

Oasis in the Desert

If you're reading my book, and you're a woman who is on her stomach, thinking you've reached rock bottom because somebody is taking your children away, I want you to listen to the sound of my voice.

I want you to stop and think. Ask yourself, 'As my children are taken away from me, what does this do to me as a mother? What is it giving me, as a mother? I present to you a new and healthier perspective - For me, it was the gift of time and space. Space to develop myself and refocus my target, which was that of getting my children back. It gave me a reason to fight with a clearer mind and strategies in order to win. This time, it was going to be once and for all! The cycle can continue, until you are bold enough and resolute to fight it till it stops.

It took me five years, going from broke and broken, to building businesses, healthy relationships with colleagues and collaborative working partnerships.

It took me five years to finally be able to hire one of the best lawyers to fight for my children's custody.

One of the miracles I love that our Lord Jesus performed is found in the book of Luke 5:1-11. We see that in order to get the attention of the disciples who were fishermen, Jesus caused the sea to dry out of fish, until he was done preaching and teaching the crowd. What happened after that, was the greatest outpouring of fish that were too numerous to fit in their fishing nets. It was only after he had finished his mission for the day, that he performed the miracle. What I love about this is the idea that Christ will cause some things to dry out if they take your focus away from your ability to let Christ minister in your life.

In my case, it was my marital commitment and my ability to parent in peace. These were taken away from me. The two things I called thorns in my life, that became a blessing in disguise.

So I want to ask you: What is that "DRY AREA" for you? Soul search and ask what blessings could be found in your dry areas. What is it trying to teach you or prepare you for? Where is the oasis in life's bitter desert experience?

If you look for it, you will find it. Look for the silver lining in every cloud. Don't focus on the cloud to let it overshadow your judgement of the opportunities being presented to you within the challenges. Instead, look for the silver lining which becomes the ray of hope that allows the sun to shine through again - because believe me, yes, the sun will shine again. I am a living witness.

Make sure that you don't lose or waste that gift. Make sure you use that time to grow yourself. I know it's easier said than done, but as I always tell the women I help... 'I have the permission to tell you this, because I have lived it'. Allow yourself to feel the pain, engage in healthy habits and don't not numb the pain.

Feel the pain, so you can deal with the pain.

I picked running, jogging, walking and traveling, as healthy ways to cope with the painful experiences.

I chose hard work as a habit, to allow myself to be a woman and feel my femininity again.

I chose not to feel guilty and allowed myself to date. So instead of sitting and feeling sorry for myself, I decided I'm going to continue living my life until I was ready to strategically fight to win.

That is what I did, and as I write this today.... I am a winner!!! Today I have my son back! My relationship with him has become closer and we cherish every moment. I'm intentional with how I spend time with my child, because I know what it's like for him to be taken away from me. I also know that one of the requirements from the therapy sessions was that his stepmother had to stop talking badly about me, which she often did. One of the beautiful outcomes of this messy painful situation was that my son got to really know me for who I am. I didn't just get to tell him, but showed him who I am as his mother, and it has made me focus on who I am and want to be to him. In as much as I gave birth to him, it's almost as though he has given birth to a newer and better version of me.

You have to see the collateral beauty in every scenario of chaos. I hope this part of my book will help and encourage you if you're going through a similar situation, to find the rainbow in the rain, and find the oasis in the desert of your experience.

CHAPTER 5

KNOWING THE TRAITS

Mr Charming can also be Mr Harming

So here is the deal...

Travel with me in your mind to this common scenario:

You may be in a committed relationship or robust marriage. You can even be with a person who says he loves you forever and always. He has professed to you that you are his soulmate - your abuser has convinced you that you are the only person he has ever loved or desired to marry. He showers you with endless gifts, attention, opens doors for you, writes poem texts that give you butterflies and even handwritten letters. He tells you there's no one else he will ever need to be with because no other woman understands him like you do. He cries with crocodile tears, telling you how heartbroken he's been from past exes who have cheated on him and hurt him...

I say be on your guard. Don't be fooled because "Mr Charming" can also be "Mr Harming". It can feel like two sides of the same coin, where he can be so good to you at certain times, then suddenly very bad to you without warning - almost as if to blind-side you. Remember, the word harming is one letter short of the word charming. The letter 'C' makes all the difference. I say to you - what you can SEE in a relationship can save you. Don't be lost in the honeymoon and butterflies of what masquerades itself as 'love'. Open your eyes and see.

Have your 'nonsense detectors' on and look out. This should set off alarm bells in you that this is a typical bait and a trap! As a loving and nurturing woman, you immediately start trying to show to him that you're not anything like those other ladies. You want to prove your love and loyalty to him. Furthermore, you don't want him to be in pain because you're a loving, caring and kind person. You feel the urge to want to "fix" him and make his burden and experience lighter. In your mind, you simply can't comprehend why any female would mistreat the sort of loving, gentle, caring, and attentive man that he is (or at least presents to be) because you would never do that to him.

The deception continues and you think to yourself....'well, after all, he loves his mother, and a man who loves his mother and sisters would certainly treat his girlfriend or wife like a queen right? WRONG! This is not always the case.

Still, you feel uneasy after some time with him. Something isn't adding up but you just can't put your finger on it. You sense in your gut or spirit that something's not right, but you're not sure what. You don't know who to talk to, or if you're just going crazy. You don't want to talk to anybody, because you don't want to make him look bad, and you don't want to look like you're 'too sensitive or crazy'. You've been told by relatives, traditions and societal norms that this is how marriages or relationships operate. As they say in my language- "Ndozvinoita dzimba, Imba inoda kushinga, and Musha mukadzi', meaning, That's just how it is - Marriage is hard work and you need to hold on to it at all costs... After all, a home/marriage rises and falls on the strength of The Woman. This mindset wrongly implies that the woman has sole responsibility, and the success or failure of the marriage relies solely on her. These are part of draconian, patriarchal teachings that have seen many women stay in abusive unhappy relationships for far too long, and longer than necessary... even to the point of even death.

The journey continues... You feel like you are on an island by yourself because you want this marriage/relationship to work. Over time you discover the more you love him and the more you try to let him know you are nothing like the other women who hurt him in the past, something changes. He has set a bar that's too high for you, and guilt tripped you into promising him that you would never be like the other women, so all your strength is spent on proving who you are not, rather than just simply being who you are. You realize you have lost yourself in the process. You feel confused, lost, abandoned, rejected, and alone. Something tells you what's being done isn't right. When you finally reach out for help from family, friends, or clergy, you discover you've been slandered and talked about behind your back to these people. It is turned back on you as you discover that they have been talking about you as if you have been mistreating the 'sweet, kind and gentle' abuser.

What your circle of friends, family, church members, and clergy don't know is that he's not the same person behind closed doors as he is in public. He is so cordial and respectful in public that people actually conclude that: "How could this charming, laid back guy be verbally, emotionally, financially, spiritually, and even physically abusive?" "He is so harmless like a big cuddly teddy bear - he could never hurt a fly". "He is such a dedicated family man, why on earth would he cheat with other women, it doesn't make sense?" This double-sided deceitful man has everyone fooled! You feel trapped. When you tell someone what happened to you, it sounds too ridiculous, because they have never seen the dark side of him. What is even more offensive is that your perpetrator has already discredited you in front of others. They may even accuse you of being sensitive, exaggerating the situation, or just trying to get attention. As a result, this chokes your voice once again because you fear speaking up about what's happening to you.

Abusers are double sided people. They portray themselves to be a nice guy to others and save their abusive self for you and your children behind closed doors. These abusers are also master manipulators. Since others have not witnessed or experienced their abuse, it is easy for them to be manipulated and believe whatever the abuser says to be true. Abusers will play the "poor me" victim card to get sympathy from others. They will also befriend or begin to hang out with family or friends that they previously criticized, and did not want you to interact with. Some of these people will believe the abuser and join in on the emotional abuse, others will remain silent, and some will show sporadic support. Those who show sporadic support for you are afraid your abuser will find out they are supporting you. They are fearful of your abuser treating them the way he has treated you. These interactions and alliances can be formed either in person or via social media. Look out for such people. They are not for you or against you, but they are for 'themselves'. I will expand later about the importance of knowing who is in your circle.

This is a typical scenario that I and a lot of other women that I have helped, have encountered. You may also be in the same situation. Take heart, you are not alone.

So, what kind of fear can arise?

The fear of not being believed

Fear that your life is changing right in front of you and you're losing control

Fear of uncertainty about the future

Fear of being punished by your abuser

Fear that someone will betray your trust in what you told them about your experiences

Fear of being on your own without a partner/spouse.

I'm here to tell you again, you are not alone.

One of my experiences of this was during a short marriage. Contrary to the fears of what my family would perceive me as, or the gossip in the community, I knew that I did not want my children to have a similar childhood as mine - observing violence at their tender age. Not on my watch! I would sacrifice all of that shaming that I knew would eventually happen, when I decided to take on the label of "divorced single mother". And so I did... unapologetically.

I remember very well, like a cursed woman after my divorce, most married friends in my community began to distance themselves from me, it was so surreal. You sort of begin to lose the respect of many, starting with your own close family, to the community, both men and women. I am not sure what this is about, but it almost feels like there is unspoken permission that some men feel to disrespect you because you are a divorced, single mother.

Upon reflecting, I believe this is why many women prefer to stay beat up and silenced. In some ways I understand their fears, because it takes a lot of courage. One survivor once told me she preferred her abuser because at least he was predictable. She knew his patterns and knew how to respond to his violence. However, the violent response of the community to being a single mother, who is divorced, was another macro level she was not ready to put herself and her children under. It is such a tragedy that a woman would rather choose violence over the shame and patronising treatment from society.

Spotting the Red Flags

In this section, we will delve further into how you can spot the red flags.

This is for you to detect the warning signs and red flags, avoid the mistakes, create a safe exit strategy plan, forgive your abuser, forgive yourself and thrive after the devastation of domestic abuse and violence. We will also explore how you can protect yourself and avoid the pitfalls of further abuse through the court system.

Let's look at some typical characteristics:

These are some characteristics, early warning signs and behaviors to help you identify a controlling abusive man. This list is not exhaustive but includes someone who is:

Cocky/Arrogant; Lies a lot; Envious/Jealous of you or others; Always thinks someone is jealous of him; Selfish/Self-centered; Cheats on you with someone else; Cheats when playing video games or games; Hates to lose a game especially to children; Has temper tantrums like a toddler; Does not respect your boundaries; Manipulative; Mean; Disrespectful; Rude; Inconsiderate; Does not consider you or your feelings; Has no goals; Gossips; Sneaky; Knows everything; Spineless with others but dominant with you or children; Bully; Insecure; Publicly shares information from your private conversations; Highly Competitive; has to win no matter what; Pins you down or restrains you to keep you from leaving the house or room; Intentionally does things you have asked him not to do. These are just a few of the common traits to look out for.

Here are some of the warning signs:

1. **Secrecy**- Is he very secretive? For example, you've poured your deepest, darkest secrets out to him, yet he has only shared the surface trivial experiences like how bad he felt when he lost his grandmother's scarf (even though she had plenty more and that was not necessarily her favorite) - something that is not even intimate or consequential. He will not open up about the deeper aspects of his life, yet he expects you to be transparent with every aspect of yours.

2. **Time and Monitoring** - Does he want ALL of your time everytime? Yes, it feels good at first but now you are feeling somewhat suffocated. Does he monitor all your activities and guilt-trip you into accounting for how you spent every second of your time? Sometimes it is disguised in endearing phrases like, "I can't live a minute without you, I can't breathe without you" or "I need to know where you are because I worry about you and your safety everytime".

3. **Attention and Charm** - Does he notice every detail, every change in hair, nails, a new dress, creepishly scrutinising your spending habits (unless he is an accountant), the slightest slight changes in your 'normal routine'? We all know that most men hardly notice the differences we make unless they are dramatic.

4. **Changed Priorities** - At the start of your relationship, did he make you first all the time, and now you find yourself playing second or third in the hierarchy of importance? Are you now an 'afterthought' to him rather than the default priority?

Once someone verbally, emotionally, or financially abuses you or does not respect your boundaries, this is a warning. This behavior is just the appetizer to their main course of the physical abuse that's lurking around the corner. When the physical abuse starts, it does not stop no matter how badly you want it to stop. No matter how hard you try to make it better, it will only get worse, once you allow it to continue. Physical abuse is the precursor of death itself, on the spectrum of domestic abuse. It's so important to speak up and do something while you still have the precious gift of life. You will find that the harder you try to make your relationship better, the more your abuser treats you even worse. He can even go as far as to tell you everything you do is just wrong and that you never do anything right.

My experience of abuse shook me to my core, because I didn't see it coming. I was completely blindsided by it. Like so many women, I blamed myself. I felt like I wasn't enough or even good enough. I felt like I wasn't worth it. I felt like I aggravated him by doing certain things that would cause him to harm me, and that if I stopped doing those things, the abuse would stop. Alas, if it wasn't one thing, it was another. I had to walk on eggshells around him and constantly watch what I said or did.

With another man, I remember the worst and shortest abusive relationship I was in. I had just met him through a respected friend, with the hope to get married again. After my divorce, I thought I had found the one.

He flew me to New York City, where he was based, and on the very first day of meeting this man, I immediately spotted the signs. It began with slight jokes on me. In conversation I would describe myself and personality, and with each characteristic, he would negate my understanding of who I was. For instance, I mentioned that I was what many called an Alpha Female, or for my sons, the Matriarch of our home. I am a powerful woman who provides and nurtures at the same time. This man immediately made slight remarks and dismissed everything I was describing myself as, and then he would make the conversation about himself.

I want to tell all young men and women this example, if you are in a new or even old relationship and this happens to you, ask yourself what does it mean when another person negates your whole understanding of who you are?

One of the tell-tell signs that you are in trouble and are about to enter a sea of boiling water in an abusive relationship is that the other party does not value and respect who you tell them you are.

That is why if you stay longer, you will find yourself lost in who you really are because this is one of the tactics of abusers - they strip you off of your sense of self, then repackage you into who they want you to be for themselves.

My "week in New York", became the longest week in my life, as the abuse escalated. Not only did this man continue to negate me and my whole existence up to this point, additionally he seemed to want to rush things to marriage, and it was yet another red flag.

Unlike animals, human beings have become insensitive to listening to our Spirit man, or as many call it 'intuition'. When you encounter an abusive partner, you know it - your intuition and gut tells you if you give yourself time to tap into it.

Two days after I spent time with this man, I remember feeling like I was drowning, and excused myself, took a walk outside his building, and called my eldest sister. I narrated some of the events, including the fact that in just two days, I had developed physical manifestations of stress, pimples all over my face, which was not common for me.

My sister encouraged me to be safe until I left, and she affirmed to me that what was happening on this trip was not healthy and this was permission for me to realize that I needed to run for my life.

Many women I have worked with will say they did not see it coming. I would like to say this may not be accurate. Usually when you encounter an abuser, you know in your gut. There are things that do not sit well with your spirit and they are very evident, but what happens is we are so interested in the idea of a new relationship and where it may go, or in my case, a single mother, one could be in a desperate space, to find a suitor and become married again.

It is important to take what I call a litmus test, and make sure it is objective. Check in as I did with my sister, with someone close to you who you know will give you healthy feedback. If you are not sure, go to the section in this book, where I point out some signs and symptoms of abuse.

My sister was right, my intuition and Spirit man were right - it was a matter of time before I discovered that this man had a lot of skeletons in his closet. He had lied about his credentials. My research indicated that he had not attended the University of Zimbabwe, making the PHD he earned in the USA, invalid. He also had a very young child, that was less than 18 months, that he never shared with me about. What else was he lying about, I wondered?

Of course I confronted him and his response was indeed violent, and that was the end of that lesson for me. So imagine, if I had moved to the next step with this man out of desperation?... only God knows what else would have happened!

That imagery of jumping from pot into the fire, is what many women, fleeing abusive relationships end up in. My African sisters suffer from the stigma that is attached to being a single mother, hence they often settle for worse partners than their previous ones.

I hope my story will set you free, my dear reader - learn to liberate yourself and abide by this mantra:

I HAVE NOTHING TO HIDE, NOTHING TO PROVE AND NOTHING TO EXPLAIN TO ANYONE. You and only you understand your situation. Move away from the need to please and get confirmation from the outside world. All the affirmation you need is right inside of you.

Once you master this secret, your life will never be the same. You will be content and have joy. I'm not talking about happiness, because to me happiness is fickle and temporary. Joy from within…. that is the aim. The kind of joy that despite what is going on around you, good or bad, no one can take away because it is within you and is not dependent on your circumstances. Your relationship status is not anyone's business but yours. In fact, I have reached a point where the question about when I will get married again is not even a topic my family brings up again. I told them that once I finished building a home for my mother and continued to take care of her as I always do, that would cumulate to more than enough bride price. So they have stopped asking me. Traditionally, it is known that most men are interested in their daughters, sisters and nieces getting married, not for their happiness, but so that the men can get money from the bride price. This anti-feminist notion is what keeps most women in unhappy marriages and unable to leave due to the issue of bride price and the obvious associated stigma of being a divorcee or an unmarried woman.

Cycles of Abuse

It is a fact of life that some relationships go through the occasional rough patch. Most rough patches may be worked out through rational discussion, arguing, a mutually respected third party or even counseling by a licensed professional therapist, but the issues get resolved. However, there are some situations that are not acceptable for any human being to endure. This is often referred to as an abusive or toxic relationship and here are some signs for you to see if your relationship is abusive:

- He controls your life.

- He constantly cheats on you - this is emotional abuse.

- You dumb yourself down so you don't seem as smart or make changes you normally wouldn't have to keep him pleased.

- He constantly checks up on you by looking at your phone, checking your email, eavesdropping, and controls where you can go and who you can see.

- He even checks up on you to make sure you're doing what he thinks you should be doing.

- Your spouse or partner attempts to force you to depend on them for basic needs.

- His actions don't show you that he in fact loves you, even though he may say otherwise.

- He verbally puts you down and degrades you in front of other people.

- He may even say he was just joking and you are too sensitive, because you can't take a joke.

- He is physically, mentally, financially, spiritually or emotionally abusive or manipulative.

In short, abusive people are not good to be around, they are poisonous and manipulative.

So, how does anybody get into this type of a relationship, and why do they stay? On the surface, the easy answer is that nobody would or should, but the reality is that they do. Abusers are very strategic and methodical. They ease you into the cycle of abuse and abusive relationships run in cycles.

There are three basic stages in this cycle:

Stage 1: The honeymoon - This is where everything seems good and there is lots of hope for a happier future. You are living your fairy tail, can't fault your spouse or partner and 'nothing could ever go wrong'. You are in 'happily-ever-after' mode.

Stage 2: The problem stage - This is where the actual problems occur. Verbal and emotional abuse are often the appetizers an abuser serves you before devouring you with their main course of physical abuse, sexual abuse or ultimately - death!

First is the tension building - During this phase, tension begins to build with an abuser who is having issues related to money, health, loss of job which may be tied to money or relationship issues with his family members. This is when verbal and emotional abuse begins. The abuser's spouse or partner falls into the trap of trying to "fix" the situation by pleasing her abuser, or agreeing with him to avoid an abusive or uncomfortable confrontation. After testing and breaking your boundaries, then the Physical Abuse or Battering begins. To get to this point, it can take any amount of time - it could be 2 weeks, 1 year, 5 years, or even 20 years before a woman is physically abused, though having been groomed or suffered other forms of abuse prior to this. I have worked with women who had been married for over 30 years when they were blindsided by physical abuse. Battering begins when an abuser feels like he is losing power and control over you. The goal of physical abuse is to beat you back into submission.

Stage 3: The Reconciliation stage - This is where the offending party makes up for what they did wrong. During this phase your abuser may show a glimpse of remorse to convince you not to leave. He may also not take responsibility for his actions and blame you for his behavior. He may even promise that he will never physically or verbally abuse you again. He may do things for you that you always wanted him to do but never did. This is to convince you that he has changed. He will be nice, affectionate, and patient long enough to rebuild trust with you. He wants to reassure you that the two of you have a strong bond that can't be broken. Therefore, it is not necessary for you to leave the relationship. This then leads right back to the honeymoon stage and it starts all over again as a cycle.

Once you know about this cycle, it's easier to understand how people get trapped in bad relationships. There is really only one stage where things seem bad. After that, they see their abusive spouse or partner is trying to do better and is sorry for what they did. Everybody deserves a second chance, right? Then the honeymoon phase is going great, they're happy again, and willing to forgive and forget. But, then the problems start again.

So, why don't people get out of abusive relationships at this point? Well, if you think about it, you can see that they already have proof that their partner can change. This proof comes in the form of the prior reconciliation stage. From an objective observer that can be hard to believe, but that's how the person in the relationship sees it. Also, they know there's another honeymoon stage right around the corner, making it difficult to exit since they have endured a lot already. Their rationale is - they might as well get rewarded for putting up with the abuse, give it 'one more shot' to save the relationship, and maybe this time he will change forever. Think of it as an addiction. The drug is the problem stage, and the honeymoon stage is the high that is felt. You can't get the 'high' without the drug. Therefore, if you are in an abusive relationship, you must break out of it at the problem stage.

Turning Red Flags into White

Apparently as women, we tend to become colour blind when it comes to seeing red flags in men. We somehow ignore and tend to excuse the bad behaviour that is clearly in front of us. Every instinct and gut feeling tells us it's wrong, yet somehow we walk straight into the mouth of a fierce hungry lion.

So what's the key to getting out?

Turn the red flags into white! What do I mean by that? A white flag symbolizes peace. You want to turn all these warning signs and previous bad abuse experiences into taking the necessary action to create peace for yourself and your children.

You have to see yourself as worthy of having peace, even if it costs you your relationship. I am not advocating for divorce or breakup if the relationship can be mended. However, I am saying that you have to value your own life to the extent that you choose peace over abuse, peace over harm, peace over fear, and peace over death itself.

Now that you know the signs, you can be ready to take action. Don't fool yourself. Get help. Do whatever you need to do to get the life you truly deserve. It will be difficult, but you will have a happier life when you do.

Here I'll also share some suggestions on how to get out if you know you're in trouble, including what you need to do to protect yourself and your children. Just as he is strategic, you also have to be strategic.

What to do when you are still living with your abuser

If you are experiencing abuse from your partner, deciding what to do can take time and leaving is a process. Here are some tips for increasing your safety and the safety of your children whilst you consider your options.

This is only a starting point. It is important to access specialist support as well, especially if you are considering leaving.

You can call toll-free the national Domestic violence helpline 800-799-SAFE if you are residing in the United States. Other countries have their own national domestic violence helplines. Familiarise yourself with it- memorise it if you have to. They won't judge you, or dictate what you should do as you know your situation better, but they can support you to understand your options and make a plan. They can let you know about specialist services in your community and help you find a place for refuge.

Contact the police:

In an emergency situation, always call 999, especially if you or your children are in danger. You can also call 101 in a non-emergency situation to report previous incidents or get advice from the local domestic abuse team.

Tell someone:

Is there a friend, neighbour, or family member you trust? Let them know you might be at risk from your partner. Arrange a secret code with someone who lives close by (like ringing and hanging up, or a blank text or ordering pizza), that lets them know you need help. You could also think about telling a professional you trust, for example your General Practitioner/ Regular Doctor.

Get specialist support:

There are likely to be local charities in your area that can provide ongoing support without your partner finding out, for example my own organisation called **Phumulani Minnesota African Women against Violence.** Many have 'drop ins', where you can access support without having made an appointment. You can phone our Helpline for referrals to services in your area, or you can look them up online. If you are searching online, remember that your partner might be tracking your search history – try and use a computer they do not have access to (e.g. at work, or in a public library) or browse in private mode and delete your search history on your phone or home devices. Find out more about safer browsing and keeping your devices safe from your partner

Keep a record:

Think about ways you can gather evidence of your partner's behaviour safely. Make notes of abusive incidents, including times, dates, names and details of how it made you feel. Tell your Doctor, so they have a record of the abuse. Save any abusive messages. These can be used as evidence at a later date. However, make sure they aren't stored anywhere (physically, or digitally) where your partner might find them. You can research more about the ways your partner might use technology to abuse you.

If you are living in nations like the United States, United Kingdom and Canada, keep record of every single incident. You know that saying, if it is not recorded then it did not happen. This is the case with domestic violence situations. Many victims fail to prove their case in court, because they are often too distressed to keep track of concise records of the abuse.

Most of the cases of domestic abuse include an invisible type of mental and psychological abuse, which can be very hard to keep track of, unless one communicates it and screen shots are taken and voice recordings are kept.

I often tell the women I work with to never take threats lightly. If an abuser threatens you, this is one more step to their taking action.

When there is doubt, record and keep track for that rainy day in court. The cumulative evidence will speak for you in court, and help the Judge to make a decision to protect your safety.

Know your rights and options:

Find out about your legal and housing rights and talk to a lawyer if possible or the free citizen's advice bureau. Explore what civil or criminal options might be available to you, including restraining orders and injunctions such as non-molestation and occupation orders, which can ban an abuser from your home. You can find information on our website www.phumulani.org or call the Helpline to talk you through it.

Financial independence:

If it is possible to do so without alerting your partner, start putting some money aside for yourself in case you need to leave in a hurry. You could also think about ways you might gain financial independence away from your partner, in the future.

Start researching this information.

Essential Documents:

It is extremely important to make copies of passports, birth certificates, court orders, marriage certificates, and keep them in a safe place. You could ask someone you trust to keep copies safe for you.

In an emergency:

If your partner is pursuing or attacking you, call the police. Also ring your local Domestic Violence Hotline urgently at your earliest chance. Call to seek help and safety.

Plan an escape route – think about where you will go so you can call the police or alert a neighbor, and plan a place to meet with your children if you get separated.

- Move to 'lower - risk parts' of your home, where there is an escape route or access to a phone

- Avoid rooms like the kitchen or garage, which contain objects that could be used to hurt you

- Teach your children how to call 911 in an emergency

- If you are not able to get out of the house, barricade or lock yourself into a room, from which you can call the police and contact friends/family or neighbors.

Once you've made the move and transition, you will feel free to breathe, go through the grieving process, and finally be good to yourself as you deserve. However, always keep the following in mind: What you've gone through or what you are still going through is not your fault - you haven't done anything to deserve being used and abused. You can't change your abuser, nor stop him from abusing you. You can't love him enough to "fix" him, to ease the pain of his past or emotional trauma. Only he can make the non-negotiable decision to stop being abusive to you, and only he can decide that he will make the necessary changes to grow spiritually, emotionally, mentally, and personally. No matter what kind of emotional baggage he carries or internal garbage he dumps on you, that is no warrant to abuse you. There is never an excuse that is good enough for you to be abused. I know that because I was there - I experienced all of it.

Today, I support, mentor, advise and speak to women nationally and internationally on how to escape domestic violence situations and help them heal from the pain of their experiences and toxic relationships. Through my organisation Phumulani Minnesota, we provide shelter and support to women who are experiencing domestic violence. You can see more of our work at **www.phumulani.org**

CHAPTER 6

ABUSE

The intangible enemy

We will now delve deeper into understanding the various types of Abuse as this is extremely important in your journey towards freedom and healing. Domestic abuse transcends race, education, socio-economic status, age, and religion.

The experience from my first marriage left me confused, hurt, and embarrassed. I just did not know how my life had changed so drastically in a split second. I couldn't comprehend how someone who claimed to have loved me so much could hurt me so deeply.

I could not understand how someone who was supposed to be my protector, could physically turn on me in an instant all because he was angry with his own personal life experiences, circumstances, and shortcomings. No one could have ever convinced me that my husband would someday become violent towards me. I had an invisible and intangible enemy that I was not aware of, and only realised when I experienced the physical manifestation of the abuse. It took for him to start physically abusing me for me to truly understand that I was being abused. Even then, I was still in denial. How could this charming lovable guy turn so mean, cold, and physically abusive towards me? Me??? I initially didn't tell anyone about how he would call me names, lie, cheat, steal, manipulate, and play other people against me, play me against other people, and force me to do things I didn't want to do.

In my state of confusion I carried shame and guilt. I tried so hard to be a good role model for my children because I did not want them to witness the abuse, or worse still, experience it too. I thought if I stayed in this marriage, they would think this was okay, especially fearing for my daughter that she would grow up not knowing her own worth and how valuable she is as a woman. I also did not want my sons to think it was ok to abuse women. My children were my greatest motivation to leave and also break this generational cycle of abuse.

I carried shame because the neighbors saw the policemen at our home too many times. I carried hurt because I could not understand how someone I loved so much and seemed so faithful and committed, could inflict such violent physical and emotional pain in the blink of an eye. So I say to women out there that are in a toxic relationship, "Speak up and Do something about it". You may not even know you are in a toxic relationship that can lead to physical abuse. Abuse is not always overt. I was being abused for years in my relationship and I did not know I was being abused until my abuser began to physically abuse me. I went through emotional, financial and visa abuse, but the physical abuse is what opened my eyes and made me realise how bad it was.

It is very important to contact the National Domestic Violence Hotline for help or seek assistance from your local domestic violence women's shelter for information, resources, and support, or get help from a professional therapist who specializes in domestic abuse and violence. Family and friends may or may not be supportive. Some family and friends may have good intentions, but because they are not professionally trained to address situations such as this, their well intended help could cost you your safety or even your life. You will also find that they may not want to get involved for various reasons or they just don't know how to help. Oftentimes family members and friends don't see the abuser as abusive because the abuser is very nice, friendly, and charming in public to other people.

To the outside world, abusers often know how to show up, in order to discredit you. For example, my mother still has a very soft spot for my ex husband. She calls him a very good son because abusive partners know how to show up to the outside people. They do a perfect job of being charming to your close family and friends, such that when you start to open up about the abuse, they find it difficult to believe you.

I would highly recommend that if you identify that you are in an abusive relationship, reach out to local domestic violence providers in your area. They have enough training to determine what is going on and will have tools to help you navigate your way out of the dangerous situation.

I did not realize that I was being abused, until a domestic violence advocate sat me down, and gave names to the characteristics of what I identified. I had never heard of these things before, but I knew that what was happening to me, was not and did not feel right. I was experiencing emotional abuse, financial abuse, gas lighting, physical abuse, financial abuse and belittling.

Once I connected with my local women's shelter and began to share what I had endured over the years, that's when I began to understand that I had been abused for much longer than when the physical abuse began. After also going to endless therapy sessions, I learned so much, including the term "gaslighting" - That is a tactic abusers use to confuse you and make you question yourself, and as a result it gradually lowers your confidence and self-esteem.

Gaslighting erodes your ability to trust your own decisions causing you to rely on your abuser for validation and permission to do things you feel you are no longer capable of doing or accomplishing. This really helped me and opened my eyes, and gave meaning and a name to what I was experiencing in order to confront it and make the necessary changes for my own good. As the saying goes, what you don't see or refuse to see, you can't confront, and what you don't confront, you can't conquer.

I had so many things happening to me over the years, but I never knew that what I was experiencing had a name. I will share the terms with you as well as more examples from my lived experiences. You will learn terms such as smear campaign, flying monkeys, love-bombing, idealization, devaluing, discarding, triangulation and many more... You may already be familiar with these terms. If you are in an abusive relationship you will definitely be able to match your experience and the type of abuse you endure with your spouse or partner. Abusers also use a tactic called 'word salad'. It is a conversation or argument started by the abuser to keep you confused with accusations, questions you can't answer, and you end up not knowing what the point of the conversation is or why you are having the discussion. This causes you to second guess yourself, doubt yourself, and ultimately lowers your self-confidence. If you are experiencing or have gone through a similar experience in the past, know that you are not crazy. There are all wicked, 'confusion tactics' used by abusers.

I became desperate for answers and a deeper understanding of my experience, so my therapist introduced me to the terms 'narcissist and narcissism' in a way I had never heard used before and how it relates to abuse. I always thought of a narcissist as someone obsessed with their looks or the classic image always came to mind of the man Narcissus, harmlessly staring at his own reflection in the water (which most of us tend to do with mirrors from time to time without being overly obsessed ofcourse). I was still confused, yet deeply saddened to learn that I had been conned. I was charmed, thought I was loved and valued beyond measure by him, only to find out that it was all a lie. The moment I began to set boundaries and no longer went along with everything he said is when I became enemy number one in his mind and the physical abuse exploded.

Exposing Physical and Sexual abuse

Physical Abuse

I shared my story earlier in chapter 3, about the physical abuse I encountered. It is one of the most common types of abuse known globally.

I want you to know that physical abuse is not about you - it is about the abuser's internal conflicts and struggles that they battle with and carry on a daily basis. It's about their insecurities and perceived loss of power and control over you. It's not about you or what you are doing or not doing. It is about your abuser, his nature and triggers.

For some time, out of shame and embarrassment, I hid the dirty little secret that this was happening to me. I would agree with everything my abuser said for fear of what he would say to me or do to me if I did not agree, and not feeling good enough because he always found a way to make me feel bad. In a flash, my prince charming turned into prince harming. For a while I blamed myself and it only was through the help of my therapist and also sharing at my local domestic violence women's shelter that I began to understand that I am not to blame. Many people ask, "How did you let this happen?", "What did you do to make him beat you?", or "What did you say to him?" They don't know any better because until they are in the same situation, it is difficult to understand. The cycle of abuse, like addiction, can be very difficult to break.

Below are just a few examples of what physical abuse can be:

Spouse/partner putting their hands around your neck and strangling or choking you; Biting; Scratching; Kicking; Slapping; Punching; Pushing you; Poking you with their finger or an object; Grabbing you by your clothing; Holding a gun, knife, bat, garden tool, or anything that can be used as a weapon against you; Grabbing your breasts or hitting your butt aggressively; Not allowing you to leave the home or force you to go someplace you don't want to go; Throwing objects at you or in your direction; Breaking your personal items; Grabbing you by your hair, and the list continues.

Sexual Abuse

Sexual abuse can be described as being forced, persuaded, intimidated, or pressured into having sexual contact with someone against your wishes. Rape is a form of sexual abuse. I always thought rape was committed by a stranger, but this can happen in a known relationship as I initially experienced from my uncle, and it can even be your partner, friend, relative, or your own spouse who rapes you. The US Department of Justice reports 76% of women who reported being raped over the age of 18 had been violated by their current or former husband or boyfriend.

The following are a few examples of sexual abuse:

Threatening or intimidating you to have sexual contact - whether this is a known or unknown relationship

Refusing to use a condom or not allowing you to use another form of contraception in the case of a spouse

Having rough sex or playing rough during sexual contact

Making you perform a sexual act against your wishes

Trying to persuade you or forcing you to have sex with other people.

I can't stress enough that when you are in an abusive relationship you have to know who you can trust and confide in. Many family members and friends have a hard time accepting and believing that their loved one can be so cruel and mean. They also have a hard time accepting that you would tolerate such things happening to you so they may not believe you or they just won't have the capacity to help you. Some may end up saying or doing things that will make the situation worse for you and further endanger your life. If you are in an abusive relationship, it is very important to contact the National Domestic Violence Hotline. They can also provide you the information for your local women's shelter. You are not alone.

Highlighting Emotional and Verbal Abuse

Abuse is Not Just Physical. As I mentioned previously, I didn't know I was being abused until I was physically abused. However, there were red flags that I didn't know were warning signs, for example, when he only wanted to spend time with me and not wanting me to spend time with my friends, family or even his family. Calling me degrading names, giving me the silent treatment, criticizing everything I wore, and picking out my clothes. At the time, I didn't know it was abuse. I just knew it made me feel awful. It was painful because I was isolated from friends and family. As an adult, I consider myself to be a social butterfly, so this just didn't feel good.

He didn't want me to go anywhere without him because he was afraid my children and I would get hurt, and he didn't want anyone to bother us. I was not allowed to do much of anything alone. He would also stress how much he liked to be with me and around me all of the time. In the beginning I was flattered and thought he was just showing me how much he loved me. After some time, this took its toll and I definitely felt smothered.

Emotional and Verbal Abuse are just as unhealthy and toxic as physical abuse. No, I know emotional/verbal abuse doesn't leave cuts and bruises, but they are very harmful to the mind and soul. They say 'sticks and stones may break my bones, but words will never do'. I beg to differ!!! Words can definitely pierce your soul and wound your heart sometimes beyond repair. Words and emotional abuse molest your mind and rape your soul leaving your spirit broken. It has been scientifically proven that Emotional and verbal abuse can cause physical health problems and emotional pain that can take years to heal. This can be so damaging that you begin to believe the negative things your spouse/partner says about you. Emotional abuse is sometimes interchanged with psychological abuse. You begin to think you are not good enough.

Your inner spirit may be speaking to you telling you it doesn't feel right, but because of love, or wanting your children to grow up in a two-parent home, and other possible reasons, you continue to stay in a toxic relationship. It is very frustrating for an abuser to brag about you to the public, yet degrade and demean you behind closed doors as I experienced.

Over time, this type of treatment begins to make you feel as though you are not good enough and causes you to lose your confidence, self-esteem, self-worth, and even your self- respect. As a result, you begin to self-blame, self-abuse, and believe you are responsible for your spouse's/partner's behavior. Emotional and verbal abuse consists of non-physical behaviors that slowly chips away at your self-esteem and self-worth.

Some examples of emotional abuse include: Insults; Belittling you; Intimidation; Not respecting your boundaries; Betraying your confidence; Threats; Ignoring your wishes; Degrading you; Constantly monitoring you; Always checking in on you; Excessive calls and texts; Stalking; Screaming; Name calling; Isolating you from friends, family, and neighbours and even from your own children; Making false accusations about you, Blaming you; Degrading you; Lying to you or lying on you; Not taking responsibility for his abusive behaviour; Attacks your character; Destroys your credibility; Publicly humiliating you through inappropriate jokes; Finding humour in your fear; Threatening your loved ones; Insulting your loved ones; Putting you down; Withholding information; Making sarcastic comments or remarks; Slandering you on Social Media; Using excessive profanity; Not keeping promises; Being secretive; Intentionally forgetting something important like birthdays, anniversaries and other important dates - Remembers things that only benefit him; Being jealous; Destroying your personal property; Breaking glassware when angry; Cheating; Ignoring you when you speak; Sulking and feeling sorry for himself to make you feel guilty; Walking away from you while you are talking as a form of control; Backhanded compliments

The following examples are tactics that are used when someone is emotionally or verbally abusing you. I have included my real life examples because I don't want you to think you are the only person who has experienced this type of abuse. I share these examples from a place of strength. No matter how lonely you may feel, you are not alone in your journey. You are loved and you matter.

Examples of Name calling includes- Stupid; Bitch; Whore; Slut; Loser; Fat pig; Fat; A bad wife; Mentally ill; Know it all; Cold hearted; Sensitive; Nut job; Crazy.

Remember a person does not always have to yell and scream to insult or degrade you. They can be experts at what I have experienced to be considered "nice nasty". These people set out to hurt you emotionally with a smile on their face and a very calm cool attitude. They say very mean and hurtful things that cut you to the core, with a smile on their face.

They can: Embarrass you on purpose in public or in front of other people; Make you feel guilty for spending time with your friends and family; Constantly tell you what to wear or criticize what you wear; Use social media to control, intimidate, or humiliate you; Blame you for their abusive behavior or unhealthy habits; Stalk you at work, home, or want to know where you are at all times; Threaten to commit suicide if you don't do what they want you to do or if you want to end the relationship; Threaten to kill or harm your pet or people you love and care about; Make you feel guilty for not wanting to have sex; Threaten to tell people your secrets; Lie on you and spreads rumors to turn people against you; Threaten to kill you, divorce you, take everything you have, or try to get you fired from your job; Calmly threaten you with a smile or insult you in a joking manner; Claim to be sick or even if they really are sick, tell you that you're the only one who can help him get well.

When you are constantly being told everything you do is wrong, you will begin to question your goals, dreams, and accomplishments. Somehow you will contemplate giving up on things that you once found pleasure in doing.

Your abuser may try to convince you that you are the problem. They may encourage you to go to counseling with a therapist or a pastor. The reality is, if your abuser has done this, he is not taking full responsibility for his abusive behavior. This is a manipulative tactic to keep you in the relationship. If he does not take responsibility for his abusive behavior towards you, the abusive behavior is not going to stop. He has to first acknowledge that you are not responsible for his actions. His abusive behavior towards you is a choice. He needs to get professional help with his abusive behavior whether you choose to stay with him or not. It took me some time to understand that abusive behavior is driven by power and control. You may be optimistic and hoping for him to change. You may want to believe him when he says he will change even if things don't feel different. You have to trust your instincts. If you don't feel safe, chances are, you are not safe. If you are experiencing any of these things or even something similar that makes you uncomfortable, please contact the National Domestic Violence Hotline.

Uncovering Financial and Social media Abuse

Financial Abuse

Financial abuse is a form of domestic abuse that can place you in a position of lacking the necessary resources to be independent in a relationship. Financial abuse can sometimes create a barrier that makes it difficult for a woman to have the confidence she needs to leave an abusive relationship. It is not always blatant or obvious, as it can be done in a very smooth, charming, persuasive, and subtle manner. In Chapter 3, I mentioned how my partner financially abused me by withholding food, money and essential supplies whilst I was pregnant.

I am going to share with you a list of tactics that are used when you are being financially abused. Some of these I have experienced firsthand. Before I share this list, you should also know that a spouse/partner can create a situation as I described to keep you from saving money and becoming financially independent. As women, some of us have fears around money or finances because we are not familiar with how to budget, save, or invest. I highly suggest you build or rebuild a healthy relationship with your money. Learn how to save money, invest your money, and definitely hide your money because in some states no matter who makes the money, the money is viewed as jointly owned. In the case of a divorce you will be required to divide the money equally. Be wise and think ahead of time.

There are different ways you can be financially abused by a spouse, and here are a few examples to give you an idea of how:

When your spouse or partner: Does not want you to have a job; Discourages you from having an income; Controls what you can spend your money on; Refuses to allow you to have your own bank account; Will not permit your name to be on a joint bank account; Will not allow you to access any bank accounts; Allows you a set amount of money each week or month; Forces you to open credit cards in your name only and charges high balances to it; Intentionally doesn't pay bills in your name to ruin your credit so that you have bad credit; Creates large amounts of debts on joint accounts without your knowledge; Makes you work for the family business for minimal to no pay, no retirement savings fund, or benefits; Forces you to work 1-2 jobs while he is unemployed yet you don't see any of the money you have worked for; Controls your paychecks by making you give him all of the money without ever seeing a penny of it; Force you to show receipts for all of your purchases but does not reciprocate that with you; Makes you account for all of the money you spend; Will not permit you to have money to purchase food, clothing, toiletries, medication, or basic necessities; Freely purchases what he wants or needs or makes sure others are provided for but does not allow you to do the same; Secretive about the details of the money, and what the money is being used for; Steals money from you; Spends money that you are saving for the child or children; Encourages you to NOT take promotions on your job or Makes you turn down promotions so your income will not increase or surpass his income; Prevents you from investing your money to increase your wealth and financial independence; Makes you pay for life insurance policies when he has no intentions of keeping you as a beneficiary. Again, this list is not exhaustive. Financial abuse can be very cunning and subtle.

If you answered yes to any of these questions, you could be the victim of financial abuse. I highly suggest that you get on the phone and contact your local women's domestic violence shelter or the National Domestic Violence Hotline if any of these things are happening to you.

I would like to also point out another spectrum of Financial abuse I have suffered in other relationships. Many women face this issue where men will target them and use them financially. By the time they steal from you, it will be too late as you would have fallen too deep in 'love'. This makes it harder to face the situation and realise that you have been conned. My advice is that as a woman, guard your heart and your wallet, especially when it comes to finances. If you are the breadwinner, and or a woman-run household, I would encourage you to seek financial advice from a coach and speak to an attorney on how to protect yourself financially.

I would call the hotline frequently, sometimes just to talk because I was ashamed to tell my friends and family who did not understand me and were very judgmental. When you call the hotlines there is no need to feel ashamed or judged. They understand and want to help you.

Financial abuse by a spouse/partner is not always about whoever makes the most money or controls the money. It's awful when I hear people say, "Oh she is staying for the money or the lifestyle." It really isn't about that at all most of the time. Understand that it is about the emotional ties we have to our abuser and the amount of brainwashing we have endured.

I can't stress enough the importance of being mindful of your money and in control of your own money. I also suggest having what I call a 'secret stash' or a rainy day bank account that your spouse or partner knows nothing about. I will put a disclaimer here: This advice is not in relation to a healthy marriage, this is in relation to a relationship undergoing abuse of any sort, that you will eventually need to escape. I write this book from experiential knowledge, to help you avoid the traps and pitfalls I fell in. Hopefully it can help you make more well informed decisions quicker, that could save your life or the life of someone you know.

I was stuck in a cycle of wanting to be transparent with my husband to prove my loyalty to him. As a result, I did not have a secret stash of money set aside that he did not know about. This was a huge mistake because when I was blindsided by the physical abuse, I had no extra money set aside to thrive financially.

If you are being financially abused it makes it even more difficult to get out of an abusive relationship. You always want to make sure you have your own hidden money stash if any of these things are happening to you.

Also, I have had many cases of women who are trafficked to the United states in order to work and pay their captor. Some disguise this with the promise of a marriage proposal or the promise of a better life. They end up abusing them and confiscating passports and important documentation that ensure the person will not leave them. If you or anyone are in this predicament, please call your local Anti-trafficking hotline. You have rights and you deserve to be free from modern day slavery. If you are pregnant and a partner is abusing you, call your local hotline who can help you.

Social Media abuse

This is the use of any electronic device that can be used for sending emails, text messages, or the ability to post. This includes: cyber-bullying, intimidating, humiliating, harassing messages or technological stalking behavior on a public social platform such as Facebook, Twitter, Instagram, LinkedIn and the like. Social Media abuse is also another form of emotional and verbal abuse, however it warrants its own section in my book as this is becoming increasingly common.

Here are some examples of Social Media Abuse: Your abuser may send you private or direct messages to force you to respond to something he has posted; Dictates who you can be connected with online; Monitors your online activity to see when you are online or last time you were active online; Publicly humiliates you in his social media post updates; Demands your passwords to all of your accounts; Questions your list of followers or friends; Checks your phone and messages on a regular basis to see who you have been communicating with; Punishes you if you don't respond immediately to his messages.

When I finally got a backbone and got the courage to speak up to him and some of his family members it threw him off balance. Since he could no longer contact me, he knew me well enough to know that if he posted something on social media I would see it. This tactic is referred to as Baiting and Bashing. Abusers enjoy playing this game. Their goal is to provoke you into trying to defend yourself publicly. The purpose of this is to make you appear mentally unstable or that everything is your fault. An abuser does not like to take responsibility. He will divert the attention away from himself and onto you.

He is a bully who seeks the support of others to carry out his attacks on you- these people are known as 'Flying monkeys' in psychology. They are the ones that do the dirty work on his behalf. This is extremely catastrophic for someone who has already endured his abuse privately. The abuser knows you are already suffering from their mistreatment, blame, abuse, slander, rejection, and isolation, so they want to see you shattered into a million pieces. An abuser delights in this - he gets a certain level of satisfaction knowing you are being tormented by the social media posts. He basks in the positive and sympathetic attention he gets from the people he has tricked into believing he is an innocent victim. The intent of this is to not only demean his victim, but to also scare her into not speaking up and telling the truth about who he really is.

If you are being abused through social media don't worry about what other people say about you. Yes, it is painful and you will want to defend yourself. Your abuser will eventually expose who he really is to the public because what he did not take into consideration is that you are not the only set of eyes watching. Some people will know he is wrong but they will not say anything to him because they already know what he is capable of doing. How do they know this? It is because they see how he publicly humiliates you. Most people don't want your abuser to treat them the way they see him treating you. Therefore, they don't get involved.

Some people told me to stop looking at his social media pages. They were giving the best advice they knew how at the time, however, each situation is unique. I did not listen. Although viewing the posts was a painful thing to do, I was able to print the posts and use them in court to show evidence of his character and what he was capable of saying and doing. These posts spoke volumes as they showed a different side of him that he did not present during our court appearances. These social media posts were admissible in court, and contributed towards me winning my case to become the legal guardian of my children.

CHAPTER 7

HEALING FOR WHOLENESS

Healing past wounds

In Numerology, the number 7 symbolizes wholeness and completion. This 7th chapter will stitch the hem and create a beautiful garment that will cover any shameful nakedness you may have experienced from past hurts, abuse and trauma. It will help restore wholeness through important keys that will unlock your life to a future filled with peace and freedom. The combination to unlock this grip on your life starts with forgiveness and healing.

Abusers have different personality types. We're frequently told to leave a dangerous situation, but they don't tell us that leaving is just the beginning. We each will experience deep pain as we start to follow the path to healing. I will show you how to make the transition to begin your journey of healing emotionally and mentally. The journal I prepared for you in the next chapter will also go more in depth to help you in your journey towards healing. Just to prepare you ahead of time, if you decide to leave you will experience guilt, shame, and even question whether or not you are doing or did the right thing. It is so hard to let go of a toxic relationship.

When we hide our wounds they become infected, contagious and passed down to the next generation if not dealt with. However, when we expose them, they can heal. I came to realise that the residue of my childhood trauma was bleeding into my adulthood and making decisions for me from an unhealthy place. Only I could change that, and so I decided to embark on a healing journey because yes, the damage was made by them, but healing & wholeness is always up to you. At some point you have to take responsibility for your own life, and as Lisa Nichols puts it - 'You are your own rescue.'

As much as organisations and shelters can rescue you physically, no amount of therapy will work if you aren't willing to walk the journey yourself. There are bridges that no one can cross for you.

Firstly, you need to forgive yourself - Do this as you come to the understanding that the decisions you made were because of the wisdom available to you at the time.

Your rationale could have been that you can't leave him for the sake of your kids, or your marriage, or loyalty, vows or financial support, fear of what people would say or even fear of death threats from him. At the time, those were good reasons to stay and hold on, but after receiving knowledge of a higher truth, it is about doing better and recognising the value of your own life and worth. Once you know better, strive to do better.

Be gentle with yourself. Give yourself a thousand breaks, and a million second chances, then pick up from where you left off. Gentle and authentic acceptance is about wholeness and making space for the bag of mixed emotions that you feel. It gives you a big container to hold the truth about your experience, as opposed to an idea that you're supposed to be living. The goal is to be whole, not to be perfect.

The strength is in vulnerability. The strength is in being able to say I'm not okay today. It is not strong to mask your emotions and live in falsehood, giving the illusion that you have everything under control.

It's no longer a compliment when people say, 'you are so strong', because of all the nonsense we are willing to put up with. This is not a healthy approach, as it denies us the opportunity to face our inner challenges that help us to get the tools we need to grow. It is disempowering as it sets a tone of expectation to not be open and vulnerable, as this appears weak. Yet the irony is that in that very vulnerability, lies your strength.

My purpose is to create an environment where you can feel safe enough to retrace your steps. Once you do so, it will be clear for you where pain, disappointment, or failure buried your hope, potential, and faith.

It is then that we realise that our experiences shape the way we show up in our relationships, and only then can we begin to do the necessary healing work to change that. As the saying goes, 'It matters not where you fell, but rather where you slipped'. In other words, when you retrace your steps, you discover the root cause of why you allowed yourself to be in the predicament that you found yourself in, that has now caused you to be bitter. Once you face the harsh reality of this, you are then empowered to take back control of your life so that you are not led by your emotions, but rather take charge of your life.

It's not what happens to you, but how you react to what happens to you that matters, and then what you decide to do about it.

I've also heard it put this way... 'it didn't happen to you, it happened FOR you'.

This is all part of practicing emotional intelligence where you change the meaning you attach to events in order to cope with them better. Rather than continuing with a mindset of victimhood, it's good to ask yourself, 'what else could this mean for me? What good can I draw from this experience?' As I said in the previous chapter, see the silver lining in the clouds that will bring a ray of sunshine in.

So after doing all the inner work with lots of prayer and therapy, I was able to forgive myself and also my abusers.

I realised that I had released my ex-husband and was no longer bitter when I found myself talking to him and encouraging him to dream again after he had hit a rough patch in life. The fact that I did not wish evil on him, opened my eyes to see that even though I am no longer in love with him, I still love and look out for him because he is an extension of my son.

LESSONS LEARNED

- Let go. Forgive yourself quickly with Grace and ease. Forgiveness is always for you, not the wrongdoer. Learn to let go and prune things and people who no longer serve you.

- Each day is like a new Canvas. What you choose to paint is up to you. You are the painter, therefore choose the colors, paint brushes, and create a beautiful picture each day.

- Establish your boundaries, and keep them firm.

- Always operate from a place of love because what you focus on, grows more. Apply love, even when people do not deserve it.

- Pray for patience. Pray also for the ability to always check in with the question, 'What does this pain have in store for me?' Find the gift in your pain as it is always there.

- Always remember that your accuser and adversary, Satan hates you and uses your mind to accuse and remind you of your past. When this happens, confront and speak life to yourself in order to cancel the negative thoughts. They say you can't stop a bird from flying over your head, but you can stop it from nesting in your hair. The negative thoughts may come, but you have the power to send them away and stop them from affecting your life.

- The end goal is abundance. It is your ability to share and improve the lives of others, whilst experiencing harmony, wellness, wholeness and peace in your own life.

In working with survivors of gender based violence for many years, I have often heard the following kinds of laments: "But he promised me that he would come through, and he let me down." "I knew I should not have let him handle this matter, especially when I knew it meant nothing to him, and everything to me". "I sacrificed my whole life so he could finish his PHD, now he is leaving me for another woman". These are regrets from women who have not yet healed and let go. They are mournful regrets from clients who had allowed others to victimize them in one way or another, and consequently to encroach their own freedom.

One may then ask, to achieve this level of freedom, how can you interact with others in healthy ways that do not victimize you? Do you need to isolate yourself to achieve this level of freedom and inner peace? How can such "healthy freedom" be pulled out of a past full of victim habits cultivated by the very victimizing tendencies of your society and your past? The answer is simple - BOUNDARIES.

The secret to Overcoming

As an empath, you tend to attract narcissists and energy vampires. Forgive yourself for allowing them to do what they did. Forgive yourself for the part you took in the hurt and rejection you experienced. Put boundaries that ensure you get the respect you deserve and protect yourself from future abuse by these 'repeat offenders'.

There are many different ways your self-esteem can be negatively impacted. Abusers can detect when a woman has low self-esteem. Most abusers will play the knight in shining armor role to rescue you out of a crisis situation as a way to win you over. You could be running away from an abusive family member, in my case it was my past experience with my uncle and a few others, and watching my father abuse my mother.

Once the abuser has won you over, he will begin to test your boundaries, starting with something small, yet offensive to see how much you will take. After a while, the testing of boundaries will be greater until the abuser knows for sure you will not leave the relationship. If you don't create boundaries the abuser will take complete advantage of you in the name of love. These experiences can be harmful and damaging to your self-esteem. It is important to know what they are, and be able to identify them, so you can protect yourself.

Boundaries are to be applied in any relationship, not only for an abuser.

It's easy to be judged by those who have not experienced your journey. Those who have not had to co-parent with an abusive ex-partner. They will be the first ones to give you 'advice', and most of the time, that unsolicited advice or opinion is hurtful.

In my native Shona language, they say, "Mugoni wepwere ndiye asinayo", meaning the best giver of advice about children is one without children. Realize that as long as one has not been in your shoes, and faced your pain, beware of the advice and or comments that might discourage and cause you harm. Put boundaries to let them know which conversations are acceptable or unacceptable to you. Handpick who can give you knowledge and wisdom about your individual life scenarios, in order to protect your own peace and mental health.

Sometimes, certain people should just not give you advice because it ends up being painful. I always questioned my one of my sisters who would give me some 'loving advice' as she calls it, but did not serve me in any way. I would then ask her...

1. Have you had to co-parent with your ex abusive partner? And she would say no.

2. Have you had to live apart from your babies, and feel a sense of no control? Again her response would be no.

Then I would respectfully tell her - we can move on to another conversation. Understand that people mostly come from a good place and want to give advice, but sometimes, it does more harm than good. Therefore, be comfortable putting boundaries on them which they should respect. If they genuinely love you enough, they will respect your boundaries.

Here are a few examples of the cause and effect of what can happen if you don't have a clear set of boundaries - this list is not exhaustive:

- Finding yourself the target of abuse in your home, church, school, or job

- Being bullied by an older person or older relative and not having proper love and support during your childhood

- Your abuser allowing other people to abuse you verbally, physically, financially, or emotionally

- Being rejected after suffering the loss of a significant relationship, job, marriage, or loved one

- Not feeling socially acceptable, inadequate or constantly needing validation

- Going above and beyond a situation in an attempt to prove your loyalty to your abuser

- Having a distorted body image and physical changes in your appearance that can cause you to feel bad about yourself, lowering your self esteem

- Feeling like you are not good enough and can't say NO as you feel obligated to agree with your abuser for fear of further abuse

- Not disclosing how you feel about the treatment you are receiving

- Doing things your abuser wants you to do even though you disagree and don't want to participate in the activity

- Taking on the responsibility of people you are not responsible for

- Losing contact with the people who genuinely care about you and your well-being. Your abuser usually isolates you gradually to trap you and disable you from accessing your support system.

When it comes to relating with people, one of the hardest things in life is to learn which bridges to cross, and which to burn.

The following section discusses the important issue about Knowing your circles and knowing who to trust.

I will pause here and share with you a very powerful analogy I heard from Bishop TD Jakes about the types of people in your life. This will help you navigate relationships better and will enable you to know who you can trust in your life. This is especially important when dealing with an abusive partner, as your source of help can either aid or further exacerbate your predicament and can actually lead to the loss of your own life or that of your children or loved ones.

This is what Bishop Jakes shared in summary:

There are three basic types of people you will encounter in your life: Confidants, Constituents and Comrades.

1. **Confidants** - Those that love you unconditionally and are into YOU, whether you are up or down, right or wrong. There are very few of them and they are in it for the long haul. A life example is a mentor - you can share anything with them and they are not afraid to tell you when you are wrong. In the case of abuse, this could be a trusted friend, mentor or a therapist.

2. **Constituents** - These are not into you, but they are for what you are for. As long as you are for what they are for, they will walk and work with you. However, don't

be mistaken that they are for you. If they meet somebody else that will further their agenda, they will leave you because they were never for you to begin with. Never mistake a Constituent for a Confidant because to them, it's all about the cause that you represent and what you can do for them. As it pertains to domestic abuse, these are the people who are with you and around you as long as things are going great in your relationship, and they can benefit from it.

This could be in the form of gifts you buy them, spa treatments, dinners, holiday trips or experiences that you include them in and pay for. However, once you are going through a rough patch and can no longer provide those gifts or experiences, they are nowhere to be found. Some are just energy drainers - they may be in the boat with you, but they are either rowing in the opposite direction, or creating holes in your boat so that it eventually sinks or goes nowhere. These are time wasters and are not deserving of your time. Do not trust or confide in them.

3. Then lastly, there are **Comrades** - These are not for you or for what you are for - they are just against what you are against. They will team up with you to help fight a greater enemy. Don't be confused by their association, they will only be with you until the victory is accomplished. They are like scaffolding - they come into your life only to fulfill a purpose, and when the purpose is achieved, the scaffolding is removed.

Don't be upset either when they are gone, because the building still stands and remains after the scaffolding is removed. In this instance, the comrades will get on the anti-abuse train with you, but quickly get off if it starts working against them. So either physically or on social media, they may see that what is being done to you is wrong and initially support you, but once they sense or fear that your abuser will turn against them, they stop the fight for you in order to protect themselves.

Expect the constituents and the comrades to leave after a while, but the confidant will always be there. The other two may not react to your problems the same way you may expect them to, but don't be upset - just be careful then who you tell your problems to. Therefore I say to you, know which bridges to build, and which ones to burn.

When all is said and done, fear not because there will always be helpers of destiny sent along to aid you on the pathway to freedom as you go through domestic abuse. These can be in the form of therapists, women's shelters, experienced advisors or a trusted friend. It is also important to consider that enemies can be propellants of destiny as well. This means that at times an enemy can actually help you more than a friend does. Enemies wake you up and tell you the truth and 'harsh reality' you need to hear in order to change your life circumstances, while friends can sometimes flatter you to obscurity. Enemies can be used as sandpaper to smoothen and polish any rough edges you have around you, and this can help you make a decision to safely quicker. Keep your eyes open and know who is in your circle.

Adversity to advantage

A story is told of a donkey that was getting old and got ill one day in the fields after a long day's work. On his way home with his master, he fell into a deep ditch. His master thought to himself, 'well I have no more use for this donkey anyway, so I will just leave him here'. Those that passed by began to throw dirt on him in the pit, and in shock of this, he just fell into self-pity. When he was done crying, he suddenly had an idea. He got up, shook off the dirt from his back and stood on it. With each shovel of dirt thrown at him, he stood on it until he eventually reached the ground level, where he could escape from the ditch.

Life can throw some dirt on you like abuse, domestic violence and trauma and you feel like you are trapped inside a ditch. But I say to you, get up and shake it off! Use that dirt to put one foot in front of the other daily, and eventually you will find yourself on top of that ditch where the ground is level again. Here, you can breathe again. Here you can press the reset button and be free. Refuse to let Domestic abuse become your undertaker. Do not give your past the power to define your future.

Dear reader, I am not sure what the root of your pain is, but like a wounded soldier standing strong and victorious, I have earned my stripes. I know therefore that I have a right to suggest to you these solutions because I have had a few encounters with pain and survived. A level of pain that I know that many would not survive from.

Sure, the fight will be a hard one, but the rewards will be so much sweeter. When you accept adversities as a challenge and not a curse, you will fight much easier. There are no obstacles, just more opportunities to learn from. Pain is a path to purpose, and you must learn how to profit from your pain.

All things are possible for an individual with determination no matter what!!!

I love the quote that says 'the journey of 1000 miles begins with a single step'.

Only you can take that first step to turn your life around.

Decide right now, in this moment that all the challenges are just that ...challenges - not curses. When you take the 'curse approach', you are ridding yourself of all power and the ability to change your situation. A challenge on the other hand, places power in your hands to overcome.

I love this analogy about the Egg, the Carrot and the Coffee bean. These are three simple ingredients that we find in our kitchens every day, but they have very important lessons to teach us.

These three ingredients display different characteristics once you subject them to hot water.

The egg starts off soft and delicate on the inside, then what happens after boiling it? It becomes hard on the inside.

The carrot starts off hard and versatile, but after hot water it becomes soft and very soggy.

The coffee bean on the other hand - once you put it in hot water, it takes over, changing the colour, taste, consistency and the aroma of the boiling water.

So what does this mean? I say to you that when the hot water of adversity is thrown at you, don't be like the egg that starts off nice and soft on the inside and then hardens afterwards. Don't let your heart become hardened.

Don't be like the carrot either that goes in strong and ambitious, and once it faces adversity, it becomes too soft, losing all hope and giving up easily.

Instead, be like the coffee bean and use that adversity to your advantage - take over and change the whole situation to work out for your own good!

Find ways to adopt healthier mindsets - programme your mind to find opportunities in every challenge. Take every adversity and use it to your own advantage!

Phoenix Rising

Legend has it in Greek mythology that the phoenix is a long-lived, immortal bird that cyclically regenerates itself or is otherwise constantly re-birthed over and over again. Associated with the sun, the phoenix obtains new life by arising from the ashes of its previous version. It dies in a show of flames and combustion, and decomposes before rising up from those very ashes to be born again.

Just like the phoenix, it's time to rise again! After facing the giants of domestic violence, abuse and trauma, don't be afraid to start over. This time you're not starting from scratch, you're starting from experience. Use those ashes to rise because now you are starting as a new and improved version of yourself - your wiser, truer, healed, healthy, wholesome and authentic self.

When we look at the process of life, remember this: It's not about GOING through these challenges, but rather GROWING through them. You need to constantly ask yourself, 'who have I become in the process?' A better version of you must emerge and the Phoenix must rise again.

I love this powerful poem by Nikita Gill

"Before she became fire, she was water.

Quenching the thirst of every dying creature.

She gave and she gave,

until she turned from sea to desert.

But instead of dying of the heat,

the sadness, the heartache,

she took all of her pain

and from her ashes, became fire."

Don't let the flames of life burn you, because remember that you are the fire! Begin to bring light and warmth into your own life and those around you.

I will introduce you to the concept of Kintsugi. Kintsugi is the Japanese art of repairing broken pottery by mending the areas of breakage with a lacquer mixed with powdered gold. This process results in the repaired pottery becoming much more beautiful than before. As a philosophy, it treats the breakage and repair as part of the history of an object, rather than something to disguise, and is hence valued and cherished all the more.

You may feel like you have been hurt and broken beyond use and repair. I want you to remember that God uses the broken pieces and the leftovers to bring abundance to your life. In the book of 2 Kings 4, we read about the widow who had a small jar of oil. Using that little remainder, God was able to instruct her through Elisha the prophet, and that jar of oil turned into an abundance of oil that provided income for the rest of her life. Similarly, Job's broken and shattered life was restored to abundance, and we can't forget the little boy's lunch of fish and bread that was able to feed five thousand people. God restores and brings abundance through the broken pieces.

Dear reader, you never ever need to be a victim again from this day on!

Take your power back

Sometimes life is not going to go your way, but instead, you have to go your way and take life with you. This is what taking back control of your life is all about.

So how do you take your power back and become free to rise again? The answer is Self-mastery.

The ancient Philosopher Epictetus wrote this about freedom: 'No man is free who is not master of himself'. Someone also said, 'There is no such thing as a well-adjusted slave'. You have to be your own master. Of course the term 'master' is used loosely - you do not have to exert power over others or hinder the freedoms of others to master your own freedom. The freest people in the world are those who have inner peace about themselves.

Simply refuse to be swayed by the whims of others, and run your life quietly. When you can enjoy freedom from expectations and roles defined by others, you have truly achieved freedom. Perhaps the best way to achieve it is to remember this guideline: NEVER EVER place total reliance on anyone other than yourself and God when it comes to guiding your own life.

For you to never be a victim again, you must take a hard look at yourself, and learn to recognize the numerous situations in which you have given others control over some areas of your life. Reclaim your own life.

If you recall from my introduction, you must already know my stance on power and control across the globe. It seems every institution, person and system is constantly attempting to control one over the other. Look carefully at how you allow or enable others to control aspects of your life.

Victimization is a process that involves both the abuser and the victim, therefore to avoid these traps, you will have to begin by redefining what you expect for yourself. How about expecting to be a victor! That is a good starting point.

My inability to obtain a job at my level due to the tabs from the mistake I made over a decade back, inspired me to start my own company. Having tried to numb my pain with alcohol, it had gotten me a tab for driving under the influence, and that made it difficult to find a job. I could have gone down the hole of self-pity with a mindset I was a victim to a system, but instead I took responsibility for my own actions, and chose to rise above that challenge of not being able to get a job. Today I am free from the strongholds of alcohol addiction, and indeed I took that adversity and turned it around to my own advantage. Within five years, I had established a successful non profit organization - Phumulani Minesotta, that serves marginalized communities and women who need the resources I once needed and was denied access. At present, I own four companies, steadily growing, whilst creating employment opportunities for others. I'm blessed to live in a beautiful house in a peaceful and quiet cul de sac location with all my children and no disturbance. This is a classic example of how you can turn your obstacles into opportunities, and like the phoenix, rise again as a better version of your previous self after enduring domestic violence.

CHAPTER 8

A NEW BEGINNING

The number 8 is symbolic of new beginnings. In the Bible, the number eight signifies Resurrection and Regeneration. Eight marks the beginning of a new era and a new order. In the secular world, the number 8 represents infinity and wealth. It signifies reaching goals and getting to a place of abundance.

With this in mind, I have left chapter 8 for you to fill in.

This is YOUR NEW BEGINNING and I am handing the pen over to you, so you write what you want your life to be.

To help you in the new beginnings chapter of your life, I have created a journal to be your guide, reflective tool and companion as you navigate this part of your life's journey.

This should take you on a path of self discovery, healing, restoration and victory. It is not intended to be cumbersome like a task or homework, but rather a lamp that will light the way for you to see. I am offering you contagious hope, that if I can do it, so can you. If I can break free and thrive, my sister, so can you. Here is your chance to rewrite your story - the power is in your hands.

With each brave step, may you grow bold,

With each new discovery may you increase in love of self & others,

With each hurdle may you discover new strength,

With each new truth, may it blot out past hurt & lies,

And with each revelation may it strengthen your resolve to break free.

JOURNAL

Take ownership of your life and decide today that you are no longer a victim but a victor. Here are some tools for Transformation:

1. *Start by doing daily affirmations in the mirror. Do this out loud to yourself until you train your brain to believe it. This will become part of your belief system and part of your subconscious and consciousness.*

    The most powerful words you can say to yourself are the words that follow the words - I AM. From the laws of attraction, your subconscious brain constantly listens and works with your life to help you become or attain what you have affirmed. Here are some affirmations to help you adopt a healthy mindset:

    I am valuable

    I am important

    I am accepted

    I am respected

    I am wise

I am free

I am loved

I am whole

I am healthy

I am complete

I am beautiful

I am victorious

I am responsible for my own life

I am more than a conqueror

I am my own rescue

Affirmations according to God's word

You may be a survivor, subjected to the strange reality of being isolated and stripped of your dignity. Spiritual practices are the most fundamental to help you cope with any challenge. It is important to remind you of who you are in Christ and I therefore created a list of affirmations for you:

1) I AM BEAUTIFUL	2) I AM LOVED
• *Ephesians 2:10 - For I am God's handiwork, created in Christ Jesus to do good works, which God prepared in advance for me to do.* • *Psalm 139: 14 - I am fearfully and wonderfully made*	• *1 John 3:1 - See what great love the Father has lavished on me, that I should be called child of God!* • *John 3:16 - For God so loved the world that he gave his one and only Son, that whoever believes in him shall not perish but have eternal life.*
3) I AM WORTHY	4) I DESERVE A FRESH START
• *Proverbs 31:10 - I am worth far more than rubies.* • *1 Peter 2:9 - I am a chosen generation, a royal priesthood, a holy nation, God's own special people.*	• *2 Corinthians 5:16 - I belong to Jesus so I'm a brand new woman.* • *John 1:12-13 - I'm a confessed believer in Jesus so He has remade me into my true self.*

2. *If I were working with you one on one, planning your life after abuse, one of the first things I would ask you to do is to assess your level of strength. How much power and autonomy do you think you have over your destiny? As I stated in the earlier chapters, victimhood can become a narrative and a habit. For you to heal completely and move on, you need to assess your level of fulfillment and satisfaction in key areas in your life. Have you ever really examined your life? Do you know what is required for you to be happy and find true freedom from victimhood? Be true to yourself and write down what comes to mind.*

_____

_____

_____

3. Next, Give yourself permission for it not to be easy to transform. Social media sound bites and even motivational quotes can make it 'sound' easy, but it's not. Sometimes you hear things like "the only person I wanna be better than, is the person I was yesterday". Sounds beautiful and it's very true, but sometimes that's a huge dare that takes time and a lot of work to get to that place. Give yourself permission to transform at your own pace. Write down your commitment to yourself.

_____

_____

_____

4. Dare to be courageous in order to become the person who can overcome any obstacles. The dare is not to get, the dare is to become.

Becoming is about changing the way you think through educating yourself, communicating, learning and growing. It's not in the outcome, it's in the process. This is a journey. Write down what comes to mind.

_____

_____

_____

10. Affirm this to yourself... I dare to show up in my life with my left overs and my broken pieces, because I believe that if I continue to do that, there is unexpected beauty for me to behold. I'm going to keep my eyes and heart open because there's another version of me that I am yet to behold. A version of me that I've always known existed.

_____

_____

_____

4. I believe that hindsight gives us clarity. Ask yourself: What is the root connected to an insecurity? When did I start embodying that? Who told me what I accepted as truth that became a poisonous part of me? What is the greater truth that I can accept to counter that lesser truth? For me, I find that in the word of God.

_____

_____

_____

5. Let your tears, wounds and whispers speak to you:

To ensure that you don't take in everything that everyone says to you, ask yourself: What is MY truth? What is the compass of my self esteem? Don't let people's words or judgements affirm your insecurities. Be willing to do the work to face inwards and cultivate a higher truth.

_____

_____

_____

6. Reflect on the times that you have felt betrayed by friends, family, a spouse, or colleagues. A betrayal is to teach you something. Ask yourself how can this work out for me? How can I turn this wound into wisdom?

Re-examine your process of allowing people to come into your life and allowing them to stay, whether friends or family. Begin to attract healthy relationships into your life by doing the work that makes you healthy.

_____

_____

_____

7. Just because someone has been in your life a long time or has some sort of authority over you, does not give them license to stay or disrespect you or your boundaries.

Toxic people are also wounded but rather than let them bleed over you, love yourself enough to leave them and distance yourself. When you are

not served love on a silver spoon, you will learn to lick it off of knives,
but I say to you, get up from that table when love is no longer served.
Don't drink their poison just because you want to be a superhero or their
saviour. I want you to pause and let that sink in.

---

8. *With this new insight, now examine your experience with others again.*
   Ask yourself: What does this relationship feed in me?

   What am I receiving from them that is so valuable that I am willing to
   betray myself?

---

9. *Inventory Check:*

   The change of seasons, and how we prepare for them, determines how our
   experience of the next season will be. In looking at this analogy, learn to
   do seasonal inventory checks on your relationships - each season, keeping
   what will serve you, and letting go of what is no longer serving you.
   Like winter jackets are for winter, learn to equip yourself with the correct
   friendships and relationships for each season you are in. Learn to do so
   guilt free. Some people are just meant to support you, teach you or move
   you from one season to another. When that season is over, learn to release
   them, lest they become the opposite of serving you. Learn to separate the
   lifetime people from the seasonal people, because mixing these two people
   may lead you to being drained. Looking in Chapter 7, put people into their
   appropriate categories - Confidants, Comrades and Constituents.

Facing The Giants

10. *Now Let us take a deeper look at where you are today with your relationship circles - be it family, work colleagues, business, friendships, church members or community-based relationships.*

Rank them on a scale of 1 to 10, with "1", meaning you do not feel safe sharing your truth and your authentic self. It is a relationship where you cannot be vulnerable at all. You love these people but you do not like the relationship as it is.

Next a "5" on this scale, means that you feel you can talk to them freely, but only about certain subject matters. You often have some rocky moments in these relationships but often resolve the issues with time.

I have learned to limit my exposure to these 1-5 relationships. I call them energy drainers, or time vampires. Learn to either let go with love and grace, or learn to love the individuals from a distance, especially family members that are toxic.

So, you may wonder, what is the 9-10 level of relationships? I call these your FIRE FANNERS, those people who make sure you keep burning to your next glory and excellence. I want you to identify your fire fanners - the people who feed your soul, and allow you to be vulnerable without judgement.

_____

_____

_____

11. *Now take these Action Steps:*

- *Celebrate your soul feeders*

- *Send them a thank you card*

- *Take time to write a heartfelt letter*

- *Send them flowers to appreciate them*

- *Give them some public acknowledgement eg on social media or at gatherings*

These action steps should be something you schedule on your calendar. I have a Saturday morning check in with my friends, by leaving them a voice note to remind them how much I appreciate them.

---

12. *As part of your soul care, I want you to establish a consistent rhythm of inner development. Take some time to write down ways you can begin to create healthy boundaries in your life. Do a page for each area you need to create, strengthen, and enforce your boundaries. For each section write down the behavior you will accept from others and behaviors that are unacceptable.*

---

13. *Also write down how you will address the unacceptable behavior for each category. For example: If someone insults me, calls me names, or threatens me, I will no longer pursue a relationship with them. This applies to friendships, family, church members and romantic relationships.*

Another scenario is if someone asks for money: I either say a firm "no", or make sure it is not more than I can afford to lose. Boundaries of any kind are very essential to the health and genuineness of your relationships, as well as your own mental health and peace of mind.

---

14. *Looking at Chapter 3 where I discuss avoiding accountability, and use the infected wound and tooth analogy, I would like you to answer the following questions: What are the symptoms that show up in my life? Are there patterns I am noticing about my life? Do I notice but ignore unhealthy toxic relationships, patterns of lack or repeat of the same situation that*

does not serve me? Do the 'dentist check' on your own life and begin to heal. This is the only way to live an abundant life.

---

15. What emotion do you try to avoid?

Why are you scared to feel it?

What do you think will happen if you feel it?

In which situations do you tend to feel these emotions coming?

---

16. What does your negative self-talk look like?

What do you say to yourself that you wouldn't say to your friend?

What positive things can you say to yourself instead?

---

17. How do I want to feel today?

What do I want my day to look like today?

How can I be my best self today?

Instead of asking yourself and your loved ones... how are you? Try asking this: How is your heart? This brings you to a consciousness where you can constantly assess your heart and address any issues that need to be addressed. Remember that out of the heart flows the issues of life. So how is your heart today?

_____

_____

_____

18. *Becoming WHOLE. Are you experiencing wholeness in your health and wellness? Take this quiz to find out:*

- *I have ample energy, vitality and physical ability to pursue amazing life experiences - Y / N*

- *I am proactive about making my medical appointments, check up's, dental cleaning, wellness check -ups, facials, massages - Y / N*

- *I maintain a consistent work out regimen, have at least 6 portions of colorful vegetables, 2 portions of fruit, Drink a Gallon of Water each day - Y / N*

- *I am active in my children's wellness as well as family's wellness - including Elderly parents, siblings or friends who need support - Y / N*

- *I schedule at least 2 hours of recharging and self-care, walk, nap, meditation, read a self-help book or tape, so I can fully live my life - Y / N*

- *I invest money and time in my spiritual, physical and emotional health - Y / N*

Based on your responses, use that as inspiration to pour more into yourself. Remember, baby steps and micro wins, will lead to the big wins! To me, becoming whole is about your physical and emotional wellbeing. You maintain your body as a temple - a gift that you were given to hold your Soul, therefore, live out your SOUL's purpose by nurturing your temple and vehicle. Be sure to thank your body daily for taking you to places you need to be and to accomplish your life's purpose.

_____

_____

_____

19. Your Spiritual Life

This is the most important of the areas I will challenge you to do an inventory check because you are a Spiritual being, having a human experience. Your spirit man is the center of what makes you who you are. How much time do you dedicate to your SPIRIT ?

Below is a scale I want you to use, to check in, and see if you rate your Spiritual Life as adequate, or scarce or abundant. After that, answer yes, no or sometimes, to the questions that follow, then write down some action steps that you will take to amplify this key area of your life. Take a moment to see the areas that are not abundant and write down some goals with a plan of how you will reach abundance levels. Remember to have grace on yourself through this process.

_____

_____

_____

Reflection				Action
My connection to God is	Abundant	Adequate	Scarce	
I take quiet time to restore my soul each day.	Yes	No	Sometimes	
I have a daily ritual connected to nourishing my spirit man.	Yes	No	Sometimes	
I feel a connection with my creator and spend dedicated time studying the word.	Yes	No	Sometimes	
I have places where I worship / fellowship and have a healthy connection to a community that I belong to.	Yes	No	Sometimes	
I have a spiritual mentor that pours into me.	Yes	No	Sometimes	

Facing The Giants

20. *Spiritual Abundance, is a sign of a healed state, because it will give you peace of mind and acceptance of the unknown. When you reach this level of abundance, your vision and sense of purpose will become clear. I believe that there is Divine Assignment for each one of us, and only when you find and meet with your purpose, will you find complete healing.*

One of the most spiritually abundant friends I had is my late mentor, Rosemary Vhurumuku. She always told me the importance of being 'spiritually sober'. `This is about learning the word of God in order to understand yourself. She always said, once you are grounded in it, you become like a tree planted by the waterside. No strange and random winds can move you. This powerful tool will make your hallmark of Spiritual Abundance because the world has a lot of noise to pull you apart in different directions. If you do not have this depth of sobriety, it will be difficult to attain Abundance in all areas of your life.

_____

_____

_____

21. *In alignment with your spiritual practice, ritual is important. What you do daily to ground yourself is critical. Practice Gratitude daily. What am I grateful for? Think about this for a minute... what if you woke up tomorrow, with only what you were grateful for today? How would that change your perspective? Be grateful for the small and big things in life.*

_____

_____

_____

22. *Moving on, reflecting on experience with your abuser, observe what types of control he enforces. For example, does he always want to be around you? Are you allowed to go to the mall alone? Or do you constantly call you while you are at work? Does he get upset that you don't always pick up the phone when he calls? Does he isolate you from your friends and relatives? Does he pick and choose what food you should eat? Does he pick and choose what movie you would watch, what dress you should wear?*

173

_____

_____

_____

23. *From chapter 6, I have shared warning signs and red flags to identify whether you are or have been emotionally or verbally abused. Answer the following questions: Does your Spouse/Partner call you derogatory names or put you down? Does he call you any of these names or similar? Does he use your insecurities about your physical appearance against you? Does he Give you the silent treatment or yell and scream at you?*

_____

_____

_____

24. *Forgive people who hurt you in the past and present and let it go. This is not an easy process. It takes time especially if the wounds are deep. You can start by reaching out and having a conversation. Do this only when you are ready and have fully released them in your heart. With some people, you will have to just settle it in your heart that you will never get an apology from them. Release them anyway - forgiveness is the key that unlocks the prison doors, only to realise that the prisoner was you. Make a list of the people, and write down your plan to forgive them.*

_____

_____

_____

25. *Write a letter to your younger self, using my own letter in Chapter 1 as an example. Dear Younger Me...*

_____

_____

_____

Facing The Giants

26. *Affirm these statements to yourself:*

My opinion counts

I do not need any validation from anyone

I can make my own decisions

My 'No' is a complete sentence

I don't owe anyone an explanation

I set firm boundaries and stick to them

I do not compromise my safety

I give myself permission to live unapologetically

I forgive myself

I live my life to please God and myself

_____

_____

_____

27. *When was the last time you made a brave decision and pushed yourself out of a comfort zone? If you could make one decision today that would change your life, what would it be? What's stopping you? What can you do today that scares you, but you know will benefit you? Write about a situation that challenged you but also helped you grow.Remember, perspective is everything - It's not what you do, it's how you do it. It's not what you see, it's how you look at it. It's not how your life is, it's how you live it. Realise that everything you need to get up, is in you already. It does not matter where you start, it matters where you want to go. So go and get it.*

_____

_____

_____

28. Write down what you want to achieve from your circumstances, past or present pain and hurdles. What would you like to gain from that pain? Write that goal down in your journal, commit it to your heart and keep it before you always. Then, map out step by step the exact course you plan to follow in making it come true. Once you have done this, you are ready to conquer all the giants and finally be free!

_____

_____

_____

BOOK CONCLUSION

In Africa, we believe in the great concept of Ubuntu, which means 'I am because you are'. It speaks of community, togetherness and serves as a constant reminder that we are each other's keepers. As the saying goes, 'It takes a village to raise a child'. It also takes a village and a sisterhood to rebirth a 'new you' after the trauma and pain of domestic abuse.

Phumulani Minnesota is that 'village' that I have created that serves women globally. We continue to support you to thrive to your highest potential as a free woman. Free to make mentally sound choices that enhance your freedom and destiny rather than choke it. You need to understand that YOU are important, you are significant and without you, the world wouldn't be. Women are the invisible threads that hold the fabric of society in place.

To end gender based violence, perpetrators must be invited to the table too.

We cannot solve it until we uproot the very base and explore why abuse continues.

We need to have open 'Healing conversations' because silence enables it. If you're not condemning it, you're condoning it, and that's how it continues.

We acknowledge organisations like 'Violence-Free Minnesota' - thank you for jumpstarting the Men's program to help contribute toward the conversation, and curate steps to change. There are many individuals and organisations joining the fight so together, we will win.

In establishing my organisation and writing this book, I have in many ways said, the buck stops with me! I am breaking these generational cycles of abuse.

Having witnessed what my mum went through, then what I experienced as a child and adult, and what I was beginning to witness through my son, I have totally resolved in my spirit that this ends here. No more shall my children or anyone in my lineage after them, suffer this cruel purgatory of abuse as long as I am still alive. Not on my watch! I am also taking steps to ensure that even when I depart from this earth, the work continues as a legacy. No woman, man or child should ever have to suffer domestic abuse of any kind, alone and in silence. I am here to help.

In my old age, if God grants me the grace to live long enough, I envision myself in a rocking chair, by the Beach, telling my grandchildren and great grandchildren some amazing stories. I would like to read excerpts from this book to teach them the lessons I learned throughout my amazing but not so easy life.

Every season I have gone through, holds wisdom and lessons that can be released as life demands. I want you to learn from my experiences so you don't have to go through and suffer the consequences that I did. If you are currently struggling, I want you to see that there is hope and a light at the end of every dark tunnel. My story should serve as a torch bearer to lead the way out to safety and a new life.

It is not easy to be this vulnerable, to share the good, the bad and the ugly, but here is why I do it. I know that anything that is kept a secret will consume you. Like bacteria, any sins we commit and hide, consume and kill us in the end. This is the same case when dealing with people. There are always some people who will be delighted to devalue your achievements and or discredit you for one reason or the other. If you are going to overcome adversities, be truthful and bring every single part of your story to the open.

Vulnerability is one of the center tools for healing yourself and others. If I only shared the successes in my story, without the hurdles and dark moments, I would not be serving another woman who may be in the dark moment. I need her to see herself in all the chapters of my life. I realised that each strand of sorrow has its place within the beautiful tapestry of grace in my life, so I choose to go through the trials knowing that they serve a purpose of greater good.

I have not always been this powerful and successful woman I am today. I was bleeding for the first part of my life, coupled with the culture shock of moving to a foreign country that is designed to make women like myself fail. I am thankful for the valley I was in because it protected me from the other beasts of discrimination that I could have been consumed by. In a way, the valley hid me until I was strong enough to climb the mountain.

Today I am able to share my story looking down the valley and standing on the mountain top because I identified my wounds, tended to them and began a painful but worthwhile journey towards my healing.

I raise up my voice, not so I can shout, but that those without a voice can be heard.

As my name Comfort denotes, I was born to bring comfort to all that suffer abuse and injustice of any kind. The word "comfort" means, 'A state of physical ease and freedom from pain or constraint. It is also the easing or alleviation of a person's feelings of grief or distress'.

So as I live out and fulfil my purpose, dear queen, I hope that this book has brought you great comfort. We are in this fight together, and together we will win!

My desire is that no girl or woman should ever have to hear the words "Scream and I will kill you", ever again. I hope that this book has enabled you to get to a place of wholeness within yourself as you literally close this painful chapter of your life and begin a new one.

Now GO and BE well! Live your best life with healing each day, and paint that brand new CANVAS with confidence.

I say this to you - "Your life is your story, be the author, take charge of the story line and do not forget to edit often." (Comfort Dondo 2021)

So from my heart to yours, here is your pen.... now it's your turn to write....

Made in USA - North Chelmsford, MA
1286499_9781838208127
10.26.2021 0815